CLIMBING
DOWN the
LADDER

CLIMBING DOWN the LADDER

LINDEN M. WENGER

Good Books
Intercourse, Pennsylvania 17534

Credits

The Scripture quotations in this publication are from *The New King James Version.* Copyright © 1979, 1980, 1982, Thomas Nelson, Inc. Used by permission.

The poem by Elise Maclay on page 72 and 73 is from *Green Winter: Celebrations of Later Life.* Copyright © 1977, 1990 by Elise Maclay. Reprinted by permission of Henry Holt and Company, Inc.

The song by Merle Good on page 168 is from *Strangers At the Mill.* Copyright © 1968 by Merle Good. Used by permission.

Design by Dawn J. Ranck

CLIMBING DOWN THE LADDER
Copyright © 1993 by Good Books, Intercourse, PA 17534
International Standard Book Number: 1-56148-079-7
Library of Congress Catalog Card Number: 93-1338

Library of Congress Cataloging-in-Publication Data

Wenger, Linden M. (Linden Milo), 1912-
    Climbing down the ladder : a teacher and pastor reflects on his retirement / Linden M. Wenger.
        p. cm.
    Includes bibliographical references.
    ISBN 1-56148-079-7 : $8.95
    1. Wenger, Linden M. (Linden Milo), 1912- . 2. Mennonites—United States—Clergy—Biography. 3. Clergy—United States—Retirement.
4. Aging—Religious aspects—Christiantiy. 5. Christian life—Mennonite authors. I. Title
BX8143.W35A3 1993
289.7'092—dc20
[B]   93-1338
                                                                        CIP

Dedication

To my own faithful wife, Esther Huber Wenger, who at my invitation and her choice, has walked with me more than 51 years the path from youth to old age. Together we loved and learned, together we disciplined ourselves and each other, together we worked and played, together we laughed and cried. We helped each other up the ladder and we helped each other down. Now after more than a dozen years of retirement we are still busy and looking ahead. We can say God has been good. We are happy and comfortable together.

Acknowledgments

I have always wanted to write a book. During my teaching years I had ideas, but never enough time. After retirement I became involved in older adults' ministries and was challenged anew to see life in its wholeness. The idea for *Climbing Down the Ladder* was born.

In bringing the idea to fruition, I am grateful for the encouragement and help of each of the following people: My friend, Laban Peachey, who encouraged me to give it a try. My wife, Esther, who not only encouraged me, but also patiently went over the manuscript, checking it for spelling, punctuation and readability. My daughter, Linda, who read most of the manuscript and offered helpful suggestions. Ruby K. Petersheim, who keyed the manuscript into word perfect to put it into workable form for editing. My editor, Louise Stoltzfus, who offered enthusiasm and friendship.

I further wish to acknowledge my parents, Oscar and Bessie (Heatwole) Wenger, who early set my feet on the upward path, and my three children, Harold, Lowell and Linda, who brought me joy, tried my parental mettle and made me proud with their own accomplishments.

Table of Contents

Preface

There are two pivotal ideas which crop up in this book either quoted or implied: "Everybody wants to live a long time, but nobody wants to be old" and "Most people are just about as happy as they make up their minds to be."

"Everybody wants to live a long time, but nobody wants to be old" pinpoints the profound ambivalence about the stages of life everyone experiences sooner or later. Those who are wise cherish life. Those who are not wise squander it. By nature everyone clings to it. And almost without exception people use it for their own enjoyment, for building up a fortune, for achieving position and power and, hopefully, for making a contribution to their community. At the end of life's stages stands what for many is the specter of old age. In our western culture, there are so many myths and there is so much bad press about growing old that it is small wonder people approach this prospect with fear and dread. It is my hope that this book will somehow shatter some of those myths and make retirement and aging something of a grand new adventure.

"Most people are just about as happy as they make up their minds to be" is both a preachment and a promise. In our humanity we have little control over our external circumstances. Life is not always fair. The forces of nature are beyond our control. Bodily afflictions are written into our genes. All the rest of our fellow humans have their own free will which they may exercise to our help or our hurt. We must give place to the customs and dictates of the society in which we live or suffer the consequences.

As Christians we believe we have been created in the image and likeness of God. We are the creatures of both time and eternity. We have the capacity of love and faith and the power of selective response to life's circumstances. It is not so much what happens to us as how we respond to what happens that determines the measure of our happiness and the quality of our person. That is what I want to say in this book.

Specifically, in matters of growing older there is little to be gained by fighting the "system"—either the natural processes of aging and decline or the artificial conventions of society such as retirement. Of course, there is a time to stand against the inequities of our current social system, but it is futile to put off our own happiness until we have reformed society. If we do so, we will never be happy. It is my conviction that even within the constraints of physical life and the conventions of our social system, there is room for meaningful activity and a measure of happiness as long as we live.

The title of the book, *Climbing Down the Ladder*, will suggest a paradox to many readers. From a spiritual viewpoint, from the stance of my personal relationship to Christ, life can and should be an ever more confident and glorious experience. There need be no decline caused by the passing of years. As Paul writes in the Scriptures, "Even though our outward man is perishing, yet the inward man is being renewed day by day" (II Corinthians 4:16b). As some of my friends have told me, they do not intend to climb down the ladder. They intend to go right off the top into glory! So much for a fine and cheerful view of life.

My aim in this book is to come to grips with the hard realities of our natural pilgrimage. While I am optimistic and cheerful, I cannot suggest that growing older does not have its pains, griefs and trauma. The aging and decline of the body are inevitable. Positions, titles and powers are passed from generation to generation. In the world of business, work and the professions, there is a time for retirement or "climbing down the ladder." Sure, it will hurt. Yet it is normal and natural, and for those who know how to fortify themselves, it is not the end of the road nor the end of happiness.

Finally, this book is largely autobiographical. I wrote it in some measure for my own benefit and to monitor my own reaction to the passing stages of life. I sometimes think of it as my final witness and testimony. However, I am still alive, and I have no way of knowing what I may still face. But I do want this book to say that life can be good, interesting, useful and rewarding. I also want to say that being a Christian can make it even better.

1. Climbing Down the Ladder

Rejoice, O young man in your youth,
and let your heart cheer you
in the days of your youth.

(Ecclesiastes 11:9a)

The ladder always shakes more
than the ground it stands on,
and what's on the ladder
shakes most of all.

"I'll tell you, it's harder to climb down the ladder than it is to climb up." My friend, Moses Slabaugh, made the statement emphatically, and I knew just what he was saying. We were talking about retirement. I thought first of several physical examples of ladder-climbing.

I remembered one of the employees in the metal shop where I worked as a young man. A good craftsman, he was sent out one day to do some work on the roof of a customer's house. He put up the ladder, went over the top to the peak of the roof and made the necessary repairs. Coming down was a lot more scary. Looking over the edge of the roof and trying to figure just how to get onto the ladder again, he lost his nerve. He made several more attempts, and each time he froze with fear. In the end, someone called the fire company to rescue him.

Tricky Ladder

I also remembered the ladder in the west end of the barn on the farm where I grew up. It went up to a little platform just under the comb of the roof. From the platform, one could service the hayfork which ran on a track the length of the barn. Of course, the hayfork did not require the services of a half-grown boy, but that ladder, made by simply nailing strips between the framing timbers to which the weather-boarding was fastened, constituted an irresistible challenge. Some misguided carpenter had nailed the ladder rungs between two studs which ran up directly under the platform, then as a sort of afterthought, moved over to the next set of studding so as to go up at the side of the platform.

It wasn't too bad going up, climbing and always looking at the final objective, namely, to ease oneself over the top sill of the framing timber and stand on the narrow platform. There really was not much to do—just savor the accomplishment, take a good look at the inside of the barn from that vantage point and think about getting down. That was different! I remember easing over the edge of the platform, over the slightly protruding sill, grasping the ladder until my knuckles were white and my fingers hurt.

I took a few steps down until there was nothing more under my feet. Now I eased over to the next pair of studding where the ladder continued downward and held fast each rung until one foot was planted firmly on the rung below. Standing at last on the solid floor of the barn, I heaved a sigh of relief. I never got stuck on that downward trip, but I sometimes wondered what possessed me to climb up in the first place.

I had no problem deciphering my friend's remark about climbing down the ladder. I thought about it often as I worked through my own retirement and watched others do the same. I repeated the remark one day in a committee meeting where we were discussing the needs of older adults. One member offered a quick response. "I don't expect to climb down the ladder. I am still learning. God is still working with me. I intend to go right off the top of the ladder into glory."

A second member of the committee was a bit more cautious and philosophical. "Well, some people do refuse to come down off the top of their ladder. They refuse to give up their offices and responsibilities until they are literally forced into retirement. Then they become bitter and feel they have been pushed off. They land with a thump—bruised and bleeding."

It Will Happen

Both of these observations have a measure of validity—some hope and some warning for each of us. Unfortunately, some of us fail to apply to ourselves or to prepare in our own retirement for the things we know full well will happen in life. In such thinking, others will grow old, but I will not. Others may suffer illness which slows them down, but it won't happen to me. Yes, retirement will come. The younger generation may take over the responsibilities of community and church, but somehow it won't affect my position of authority and influence among them.

This failure or inability to face the realities of life can be the source of great unhappiness and bitterness. Simply put, it is the refusal to climb down the ladder when our turn is finished. We do not prepare for retirement. By some mental gymnastic, we push away the thought of it. We neglect making closure of affairs in office, business or profession. Perhaps, we have not cultivated any hobbies, nor planned any second career to keep going emotionally. We may not even have given thought to our financial needs and resources in the years of retirement which lie ahead.

When retirement does come, we feel pushed off the ladder. Rather than coming down rung by rung with dignity and purpose to achieve a safe and happy landing, followed by years of useful and satisfying retirement, we spend time sulking and complaining about the unfairness of our "dismissal," and the emasculation of the seasoned talents of older persons in general. We usually manage to make ourselves thoroughly unhappy and do little to add to the enjoyment of others.

I began this discussion with the remark of my friend, Moses Slabaugh, about it being harder to climb down the ladder than to climb up. That, as an astute observation on life's pilgrimage, I do not deny. It is not easy to give up a job into which we have poured heart and soul. It is not easy to surrender a prestigious position and the control we have been accustomed to for years. Nor is it easy to acknowledge the diminishing physical powers which come with the years. However, there are gracious ways of meeting and accepting these realities which, in turn, will greatly enhance the possibilities of happiness and usefulness in our older years.

May I Get Off at the Top?
The figure of going off the top of the ladder into glory is not at all foreign to the purposes of this writing. The figure of the ladder is, for the most part, a way of talking about human achievements which we must ultimately relinquish to those who follow in our footsteps.

Going off the top of the ladder does reinforce a very valid concept about aging. Old age can be a happy and rewarding time. Retirement does not diminish personhood. It does not mean inactivity unless we choose it to be that way. We will not be "turned out to pasture" unless we are willing to go. The old adage that one can lead a horse to water but cannot make him drink may have some application here.

True, policies beyond our control may require retirement from a longtime profession or job, but that need not force us into inactivity nor out of opportunities for continued growth or significant service. As my friend from the committee said, "God is not finished with me yet." However, much like coming down that ladder in the end of the barn of my boyhood days, happiness and usefulness after retirement may require some concentrated thought and attention.

Examine your post-retirement options. You may not need to retire "cold turkey." It might be possible to remain part-time in your employment or to become a consultant. Now may be the time to begin a business of your own or to give prime time to a long-deferred hobby which might itself become a second career. Now may be the time for renewed personal growth and development. Now there is freedom to attend classes offered by the local college, time for serious reading and writing, time for travel (not necessarily a trip to Europe or the Far East).

For adding joy and purpose to life, there are abundant service opportunities. Search for them in the area of your own expertise, whether it be professional, clerical or in the trades. In fact, it may be said that we live in an era of voluntary service. Serving others, making the world a better place, provides a sense of fulfillment, a sense of usefulness, even a sense of being in control. Serving others in the name of Christ further gives one the sense of the supreme worth of life.

I have known persons who made even their years of physical decline fruitful by their labors of love and prayer. They visited, wrote letters or used the telephone to minister to others. They carried long lists of people and causes for whom and for which they prayed daily or at least regularly. To the end, their lives were radiant and satisfying. In this sense I understand and agree with my friend who says he expects to go off the top of the ladder into glory.

I also know exactly what my friend, Moses Slabaugh, meant when he said, "It is harder to climb down the ladder than it is to climb up." Our American culture has produced a generation of ladder climbers. Success is the name of the game. Parents urge their children into Little League and constantly implore them to do better. Children are sent to preschool and head start in order to get them on the way to a prestigious college. They have little time to dream, to fantasize and to lie on their backs in the grass wondering at the cloudscapes, the trees and the butterflies. By high school age, parents and teachers are encouraging them to "be somebody," to get ahead in athletics, scholarship or the social scene. To try to give it a good name, children and young people are encouraged to strive for excellence.

The Pursuit of Excellence

Be assured, I have no fault to find with the pursuit of excellence in its proper time and place. I firmly believe that God intends for us to make the most of the talents with which He has endowed us. He intends that we make our contribution to the enrichment of our fellows, that we add something to the world's store of good and counteract the evil that pursues us, that we somehow justify our having lived. Unfortunately, in our society the pursuit of excellence has too often been prostituted into the drive to get ahead. People are judged by what they have rather than by what they are, by their possessions rather than by their person.

In America we tend to identify persons with their positions.

She is professor of chemistry at Brown College; he is pastor of First Baptist Church of Troy; she is quality control engineer for Black and Sons; he is master carpenter for Gray Construction Co.; she is vice-president of sales for Green Limited. These positions not only provide identity, but they also carry with them a certain prestige and power. They provide a basis for "bragging rights." When we retire from these positions, we are likely to feel that we have lost something of our identity. Our personality has somehow been diminished.

When strangers meet at a luncheon or on a plane, the first question is, "What is your name?" Should they be Mennonite or members of some other close-knit ethnic group, the questioner often follows with, "And who are your parents?" which is really only an extension of the first question. The second important inquiry is, "What do you do?" This is the real identifier and begins to give people place and position. While everyone needs a name for the convenience of the post office, the social security administration and the bureau of vital statistics, the name itself will not spark response between the newly-met unless by some far chance it uncovers a connection on someone's family tree—our own or that of a friend.

Instead, in our culture, what we do gives us individuality and place. It is usually sufficient base upon which to build continuing conversation. What we do establishes our social position and gives us importance and even power. An office or profession places us somewhere on the ladder of fame and influence. Unfortunately, this does not always clearly indicate our actual merit or the quality of service rendered to those around us. Nevertheless, persons are identified by position in the eyes of those about them, as well as in their own eyes.

In my own case, I was a college professor and a bishop in the Mennonite church. I found particularly that the office of bishop carried with it a measure of respect and even fear. It evoked certain expectations which I was not always able to fulfill. The awe that I sometimes sensed for my office was out of keeping with my own perception of my personality—a mild, kindly and rather timid individual. It did help me to keep in perspective the distinction between Linden M. Wenger, the bishop, and Lindy Wenger, the person—a distinction which served me well when it came time for me to retire.

This tendency to identify persons with position was well illustrated for me when I went on a study tour of the Holy Land under the direction of New York University. The group consisted of seminary and college teachers of Bible from diverse religious backgrounds. Among them were a Catholic priest and two nuns. I drew the priest for a roommate. We became friends and learned a great deal from each other. He seemed duly impressed to learn that he was sharing his room with a bishop. I was somewhat amused with his attempts to climb the ladder in the hierarchy of his own denomination. He eagerly communicated to his superiors back home his good fortune in being thus identified with a bishop.

At the time I was wearing the traditional Mennonite plain coat, so along with the priest and the nuns, we made up a foursome immediately identified by our garb. For this and whatever other reasons, we established a certain rapport for the trip. There was an evening when our entire group had an audience with Archbishop Hakim, then the reigning prelate of the Greek Catholic Church in Israel. Hakim was arrayed for the occasion in all the regalia of his office (at least it looked that way to me). His greetings were friendly but reserved. As he greeted the younger nun, he took occasion to chide her that the dress adopted by her particular American order was too short to meet his standards. When it was my turn to shake hands with the Archbishop, I simply gave my name without mentioning any credentials. My Catholic friends quickly informed the Archbishop that I was indeed a Mennonite bishop. Hakim looked me over from head to foot and then remarked evenly, "Your habit is very simple." I was not quite sure whether the remark was a compliment or a put-down, but I felt slightly uncomfortable. Clearly, I was in the presence of a man who knew how to make use of his office and titles.

I learned from this and many subsequent experiences that people use their positions to gain personal advantage, to demand attention or to get their own way without the necessity of logically vindicating their course of action. This is ladder-climbing in a bad sense, and those who do it are the ones who hate most to climb down when their time comes. "Professional" ladder-climbers learn to use any of a bag full of tricks—getting near the celebrity who is being interviewed, appearing in the right spot when pictures are being taken, asking questions at the right time. Some people may do these things almost unconsciously; others, of course, with design. The Apostle Paul in his Corinthian letter, however, suggests a "more excellent way" to personal fulfillment.

When Pursuit of Excellence Goes Astray

Most of us spend a good part of our lives climbing the ladder. Parents encourage their children to do their best, to bring honor to the family name. Teachers urge their students to strive for excellence, to make a mark for themselves in the world. Students are taught to hone their skills with care. This is the way to success, to financial reward, to recognition, to position and power and, finally, to the sense of personal achievement and worth. Though the philosophy is sometimes challenged, our educational system seems to be set up in a way that fosters a fierce competitiveness which not only calls forth the utmost effort, but makes getting ahead the primary goal.

I make no apology for the fact that for twenty-three years

of college and seminary teaching I encouraged my students, even young pastors, to strive for excellence, to cultivate their God-given talents for the glory of God and the service of others.

Striving for excellence goes astray when success is equated with personal achievement, financial gain and private power. To make money by any and all means is too often the American goal. It goes astray when fulfillment of purpose becomes self-fulfillment.

There is a school of psychology which says you owe it to yourself to become all that you can be, to enjoy all that you have the capacity to enjoy. If that effort infringes on someone else's rights—too bad. If it conflicts with solemn promises you have made to your spouse and children—too bad. If it leaves no time for service to the community and church— again, too bad. Climbing the ladder becomes wrong when it is done at the expense of others, when we climb up by pushing others down. The Bible teaches us a truth that personal ambition fails to understand. Jesus said, "Whoever desires to become great among you, let him be your servant" (Matthew 20:26b).

Jesus, in the parable of the talents (Matthew 25:14-30) and the parable of the pounds (Luke 19:13-24), teaches the importance of cultivating the gifts which God has given us (striving for excellence). In the parable of the rich fool (Luke 12:16-21), He shows the folly of using God's gifts and talents only for self-satisfaction.

Ladder climbing may be done honestly and with noble purpose, or it may be done selfishly. In any case, it is a normal part of life. Because so many of us are intent only on climbing, we fail to reckon with the fact that some day we will reach the top of our personal ladder. Sooner or later (and it customarily seems sooner), whether for reasons of physical decline, public law, company policy or simply because younger feet are clambering on the rungs below us, we will need to relinquish our position on the ladder. Our place and our responsibilities will be taken over by others. We will need to surrender position, responsibility, authority, power and probably titles to someone else.

Like it or not, it is a rule of life and a fact of history. That it will not be done without pain is also normal. It will be much the same whether we have done our climbing honorably or selfishly. Retirement for most people seems to come rather abruptly, even though we have tried to think ahead and to prepare ourselves for it. Climbing up our ladder has been a long process. We always had something to which we were looking forward. We savored each small victory, each advancement, with pleasure. We probably had forgotten most of the disappointments and embarrassments along the way. But retirement comes with a sudden finality that often leaves us wounded and wondering.

Deciding to Come Down

The chapters which follow will explore the ways in which we may learn to face the facts and realities of life as they relate to retirement and growing older. I intend to bring a Christian perspective to the whole of life, to show that the sunset years can be beautiful and satisfying.

It is possible to look ahead, to prepare for retirement economically and physically. However, to fortify ourselves psychologically and spiritually for the changes which advancing years are sure to bring may be more difficult. We can and must realize that "coming down the ladder" is not the end of life or growth or usefulness or joy. The sun still shines and life can be full of peace and contentment. A certain elderly letter writer reminded a good friend that "Godliness with contentment is great gain" (I Timothy 6:6).

For twenty-three years I was teacher of Bible and philosophy at Eastern Mennonite College and Seminary. They were extremely busy and good years. At the same time I carried responsibilities in the church. During the second half of my tenure, I gave up most of my classroom teaching in favor of administration. Among other things, I was Assistant to the President for a time and worked closely with Myron Augsburger, who was then President. I learned to know Myron rather well. He could make decisions and administer with gusto. But underneath he had a tender heart. He hated to give people bad news. As I neared the time for retirement, I knew full well that someone needed to broach the subject. Normally, it was Myron's task. I decided to take the initiative and spare Myron what I hoped was an unwelcome duty. One day when I had an appointment in his office, I said, "Now, Myron, you know that before this school year is over, I will be sixty-five. I expect to be released from all duties by next year. I still have a lot of work to do in the church which I feel I may have neglected during the press of academic responsibilities here."

Myron smiled. There was a relaxed atmosphere between us. It was easy to plan the closure of my assigned responsibilities, easy to provide orientation for my assigned successor. I was already several rungs down my ladder.

2. Facing the Inevitable

"I am this day eighty-five years old.
As yet I am as strong this day as I was
in the day that Moses sent me." —*Caleb*

(Joshua 14:10b-11a)

Pity those people
who keep running
from something
that isn't after them.

My wife, Esther, and I have gotten somewhat addicted to the yearly Senior Adults Retreat at Laurelville Mennonite Church Center. The first time we were there, we walked into the get-acquainted assembly, took one look at the people gathered there and said to ourselves, "What are we doing here with this crowd of old people?" We soon found out. We found that we belonged. It is, by and large, one of the most upbeat groups with which we regularly associate. Never mind the canes and crutches or the occasional wheelchair. These people trade stories about hip and knee replacements like youngsters trade baseball cards. Many of us have looked death in the face and come away unafraid. So we just have a good time of fellowship, tell old people's jokes, laugh at ourselves, laugh with each other and sympathize a bit with friends over our mutual aches and pains.

Of course, we always also have a speaker who challenges us with opportunities yet to be grasped, things yet to be done. It is a group that has made peace with the idea of aging.

The first year we attended, the moderator announced that Paul and Edna Shank, who had played a major part in the planning of the retreat for a number of years, would not be present the next year. They were leaving their home in Indiana for an assignment in Illinois. The announcer seemed momentarily at a loss for words when he tried to say what they would be doing. Then he got it, "They will be working with the aging!" Of course, I knew there was a church-sponsored retirement center in the area. I could easily imagine what they might be doing, but it struck me as rather amusing. Inside I was chuckling and saying to myself, "Who isn't working with the aging?" The only professional I know who doesn't work with the aging is the undertaker whose clients have stopped growing older.

When my Aunt Katie Wenger had her eighty-fifth birthday, our pastor gave her a bit of recognition in the morning church service. "How does it feel to be eighty-five?" she was asked. Without a moment's hesitation, she replied, "It feels real good. If I wasn't eighty-five, I would be dead." Many of the people I describe in this book are much more alive, exhibiting more joy in living, than many persons half their age.

The Absurd Cult of Youth

In our American culture, we have had an absurd love affair with youth—what I call a cult of youth worship. First, there is the physical infatuation with youth—the sparkling eye, the smooth skin, lustrous hair, correct measurements. Millions of dollars are spent annually by American women and men on shampoo, skin lotions, massages, diets and sundry beauty treatments designed to make themselves feel young and to stay young-looking regardless of age. The idea is, first of all, to meet the expectations of the media, and secondly, to appeal to the opposite sex while becoming the envy of the same sex. Slick magazine ads and television commercials in living, sometimes lurid, color hard-sell the idea that youth, beauty, glamour and happiness may be purchased with money, and life is not worth living without it. The implication is that when youth is gone, life and happiness are also gone. Don't believe it!

Of course, the lustful infatuation with the youthful body is not new. Ancient kings and great men were prone to add to their store of wives and concubines the most beautiful maidens of the realm—to satisfy their own sexual lust and reinforce the impression of their own youth and vigor. The search for the fabled fountain of youth is almost as old as the history of humankind. The famous Spanish explorer, De Soto, thought it might be found in America. Apparently millions of people still think so. A current television ad pictures a smooth-skinned, fair-haired, starry-eyed female saying, "There is a part of me that says, 'Why not just grow old gracefully,' and then there is the real me ..." Someone should tell the "real me" that lotions, shampoo and bubble baths not withstanding, we all grow old, not just some of us, but all of us. As Aunt Katie implied, the only alternative is to die young.

The second thrust of this cult of youth worship is aimed at the psychological and intellectual. A few years ago it was the dictum of the Yuppie culture that no one over thirty could be trusted. Anyone past that fictional age was out of touch, could not possibly know what was important or what was going on in the world. Anyone over thirty had lost the zest for life, the capacity for fun, the zeal for adventure, the ability for adaptation and the intellectual acuity to come to grips with the world's problems.

In most respects this second aberration is even more misguided than the infatuation with physical beauty. According to its standards, even the famous and foolish Alexander the Great had outlived his time when he died at thirty-three. Nothing is more adequately documented than the fact that the remembered achievements of humankind (sports excepted) are almost exclusively the province of those above the magical age of thirty.

In the ancient Jewish economy, a man did not reach his full maturity until age thirty. Interestingly, Hebrew priests retired from the priesthood at age fifty, but not to a life of inactivity or without influence. Having served time in the duties of this religious office, the priest was now free to attend to the family fortunes, to study, write or pursue some other project. Most of all, he enjoyed a place of honor and prestige, serving as an elder in the councils of the community, sitting at the gates of his city.

In our own culture, until very recently, we believed the middle years of life—thirty to sixty or seventy—were the years of accomplishment, responsibility and power. The years before were preparatory, the years beyond were discretionary—years to be used as seemed good—keep on working, slow down gradually, serve as an elder statesman, but still retain authority. It was a time to enjoy leisure activities, according to choice. Only those of us under eighty or eighty-five spent all our working years knowing we faced mandatory retirement at sixty-five.

The Retirement Bogy

Certain misconceptions have been passed along with this mandatory retirement package—the notion that opportunity is gone, that the individual is out of circulation and that intellectual powers have somehow diminished. Taken away at retirement is the familiar and no doubt comfortable place and routine of work; the regular source of income which afforded financial security and a certain title or position which gave identity and status. The notion that one's intellectual powers have been thereby diminished is a cruel hoax. The feeling that opportunity for useful and happy living, even for significant accomplishment, is past is likewise an unfounded delusion. Retirement does not take away the opportunity for independent business ventures, for political involvement, for literary, artistic or religious achievement.

To discover the significant accomplishments and contributions which humankind now cherishes and honors of persons in their later years, one needs only to take a look. Grandma Moses took up painting at seventy-eight when her fingers became too stiff for needlework. She finished her last contracted illustrations at one hundred. Michelangelo was seventy-one when appointed chief architect for St. Peter's Cathedral in Rome. He worked on it for the next eighteen years until his death at eighty-nine. During that time, he did some of his most notable work, including his finest poetry. Noted American architect, Frank Lloyd Wright, began his most creative period of work at age sixty-nine and continued unflaggingly until his death at ninety-one. Among his best-remembered works are the beautiful and innovative Falling Waters, mansion of the wealthy Kauffman family at Bear Run, Pennsylvania, and the equally innovative Guggenheim Museum in New York City. The great Russian writer, Leo Tolstoy, experienced a spiritual conversion at fifty-two. Thereafter he devoted his talents to moral, social and spiritual themes, doing his most sensitive writings shortly before his death at eighty-two.

These examples could be multiplied. Perhaps you are waiting impatiently to say, "These are exceptions, not the rule."
If these are the exceptions, whose fault is it? Rather, these
should be seen as the examples and the challenges. More and
more people are living to an older and older age. With more
and more prime time of reasonable physical health and unim-
paired intellectual faculties being given to this generation
between retirement and death, why should there not be years
of happy and satisfying accomplishment?

It is not to be expected that after retirement everyone will
suddenly become gifted in something they were not doing
before, although it could happen. The point is, retirement does
not take away your gift nor diminish your person. You simply
find a new outlet for your gift or training. You have an
opportunity for latent talents and desires within you to flourish
in accordance with your strength.

Growing Older Is Normal

Having dispensed with at least a few of the goblins and
gremlins which the American youth culture has imposed upon
us, let us look at the hard facts. We are all growing older. No
fountain of youth may be found, not in the beauty parlors of
America nor in the mountains of Tibet. The only fountain of
youth we will ever find occurs within ourselves—in the will
and wisdom to renew our own spirit and to take care of the
body which our Creator has given. The Bible circumscribes
the length of human life. "The days of our lives are seventy
years, and if by reason of strength they are eighty years, yet
this boast is only labor and sorrow; for it is soon cut off, and
we fly away" (Psalm 90:10). Yes, when the Psalmist made his
observation or dictum (whichever you choose to call it), there
were people who lived longer than eighty years. Today we
would call his pronouncement "rule of thumb" or average. For

most of the world's history and in most countries, the average life expectancy has been much less than this.

One of the phenomena of our own time has been the increase in life expectancy for people who live in North America. Statisticians point out that the overall increase in life expectancy results largely from the development of medical science which has drastically reduced infant mortality and conquered many of the bacterial and viral diseases which devastate children and youth. But the statisticians must also note that the over-eighty-five bracket is the fastest growing segment of our population and the seventy to eighty-five population has also grown in similar proportions.

Over all, life expectancy in the United States is currently 74.7 years, a few more for women and a few less for men. This does not indicate much change from the observation of the Psalmist. The intervening figures on life-expectancy, how-ever, point out clearly that today the portion of our population reaching the accepted retirement age of sixty-five has greater and growing expectations for more years of life, service and enjoyment, thanks to the advances of medical technology and improved health consciousness. In 1990 persons reaching age sixty-five had an additional life expectancy of 17.3 years (19.0 years for females and 15.3 for males).[1] That is a nice lot of retirement time.

So many good things have been added in recent years with the prospects of longer life, better health and meaningful activity that I am having a hard time getting to the cold hard facts. But they are still there.

The Psalmist made an interesting observation. The days of our years were to be threescore and ten, but if by reason of strength they became fourscore, yet was their strength labor and sorrow. What did he have in mind? Was it the progressive decline of physical strength and vigor, loss of eyesight and hearing, for which there was little help in that day? Was it the increasing difficulty in walking—the chief means of getting from place to place? Was it the periods of pain and illness for which there were no doctors or hospitals? Or was it the loss of friends and family—his peers on whom he depended for social contact? Was it that enclosing sense of loneliness which then and now plagues those who outlive their familiar companions? I don't know, but the then-and-now comparisons are interesting.

On the average those who reach sixty-five may now expect to live another seventeen years. That is not exactly the same as saying that seventeen years have been added to the American life span, but the figures do indicate that more and more people are living longer and longer. This does not diminish in the least the fact that we are all traveling toward the grave. We know of only two persons in the world's history who have escaped dying—Enoch and Elijah. That makes our mathematical probabilities rather slim!

Ever since we were first married, my wife and I have said to ourselves occasionally, "Maybe we will live until the Lord returns. Then we will never be separated from each other by death." It is a nice thought. One that grows out of our particular brand of Christian faith—the belief that Jesus is coming again and that His own will be caught up into glory without dying. It is not something, however, that we can figure into the probability statistics of our life span.

Would You Like to Know?

I often wonder about King Hezekiah. The shadow of the sun going back fifteen degrees on the dial of Ahaz was a sign to him that he would recover from his present sickness and fifteen years would be added to his life. Hezekiah must have said, "Whoopee, another fifteen years; that's a long time."

Then it was fourteen, then thirteen, then... Hezekiah could have become quite morbid as the time wound down. I really think I prefer to live without knowing—to say in Christian faith, "My times are in your hands" (Psalm 31:15a).

At the time of Lyndon Johnson's death, I read in the news accounts that some years before he had done a very detailed computer analysis of his life expectancy, taking into account the life span of his parents and grandparents for several generations, their known ailments and diseases, their good and bad health habits and, of course, the habits of Lyndon Johnson himself. The analysis came up with the probability that Johnson would die in his sixty-fifth year—and he did. I sometimes wonder if he died from his physical ailments or from a bad case of computeritis.

When I first studied psychology, one of my teachers loved to tell the story of the aged woman whose parents and several brothers and sisters had all died in the month of February. The woman came to look upon February with dread and fear which increased with each passing year. Finally, as one February approached, she began to say to her friends, "If I can just make it through February, I'm sure I will live for another year." She didn't.

A great difference exists between a morbid psychotic fear of aging and death and a wholesome recognition and acceptance of life's times and stages. The writer of Ecclesiastes observed, "There is a time to every purpose under heaven; a time to be born and a time to die...a time to weep and a time to laugh...a time to get and a time to lose." Maturity and peace of mind lie in recognizing and accepting the sequential stages of life, each with its own purpose and responsibility. It will not help us to fear death or to deny that the last stage of life includes aging and death.

Stages of Life

Childhood was meant to be a time of happiness and security, a time to develop physically, to learn to relate to other people, to find personhood and confidence. In American culture, we have tended to short-change childhood, pushing children prematurely into a fiercely competitive world, expecting of them achievements beyond their years, never allowing them time to dream. Worse yet is the breakdown of family life—divorce, broken homes, single parent households. So often children are denied the privilege of both male and female role models—the opportunity of seeing both mother and father in loving, secure and confident relationship, working together to meet life's joys and troubles. Childhood experience is the seedbed of security or insecurity in old age. Even the experience of religious conversion will not necessarily erase the effects of an unhappy childhood where hurts and hostilities have been solidified into anger and mistrust. Only the experience of learning to forgive and be forgiven, possibly with the help of Christian counseling in which the person learns to understand others and to accept his or her own pain, erases such scars.

Youth is the time for final physical maturity, for education and intellectual development, for the choice of a career and likely the choice of a mate. There is the separation from parental home and the assumption of full personal responsibility.

For my own purposes, I will divide adulthood into three stages: young adults, middle adults and older adults. The young adult stage, say from the mid-twenties to the mid-forties, is the time for climbing the ladder, the time of physical and intellectual vigor. This is the time to seek advancement in one's chosen trade or profession, the time to become established in business, to rise in the corporate structure, the time when one begins to taste power and influence.

The middle adult years, from forty-five to sixty-five, are normally the years of power and achievement, the time to make money, to receive titles, to assume an identity that assures one a place in society, perhaps history. These things in themselves can be either good or bad. Those who achieve may serve their family, their community and their church well. Too often, in our society, striving to achieve may make men or women self-centered and forgetful of others—even family.

I am not speaking only of "big people" and "big achievements." We all want to climb the ladder, to achieve a measure of excellence. Whether we are farmers, carpenters, salespersons, secretaries, teachers or housewives, we always strive for achievement in our own sphere of activity and influence. We just tend to forget that the time comes to climb down and give room to the next generation, our own children.

The third stage of adulthood naturally is now defined by retirement, when, at the very least, there must be some retrenchment of activities and some adjustment of life. The possibilities for life beyond retirement are the focus of this book. However, this stage of life does not depend solely upon the stroke of a birthday party.

Probably the first reminder of our mortality for most of us is the age-wearing of our own bodies. We age at different rates, and medical scientists differ in their conclusions as to what is normal. Common wisdom agrees that the human body reaches its peak of strength at about thirty. This may continue with the individual taking little notice of decline for twenty years or more. At about fifty, those of us who engage in physical labor begin to notice that we tire more easily and it takes us longer to bounce back. Interestingly, in physical feats the middle-aged person can often fend off the younger person of superior strength simply by the endurance and experience which the older one possesses.

It Happened to Me

When I was in my middle thirties, our family moved to the West Virginia hills where I was to be pastor of several small churches and make a living by farming. I did some hunting and hiking on the side. We often entertained weekend campers and hikers from Eastern Mennonite High School and College. When we started for a hike, the first order of the day was to wear those rambunctious kids to a frazzle. Then we could settle down to observing nature and enjoying the mountain terrain. Only once in the ten years we lived in the hills did I meet a kid who so much as gave me a scare. Would I try it now? No way! I moved on to teaching and a more sedentary life. More than that, forty years have gone by. My knees, my lungs, my muscle tone, my stamina (lack of it) tell me those times are past. Oh, Esther and I still walk, but we prefer level ground. Since she suffers from allergies and lately asthma, we do most of our walking inside in the mall where we can tick off two miles at a good pace.

Advantage of Experience

Remember the story in II Samuel 2 of the war between the house of Saul and the house of David. When the army of the house of Saul was defeated and fleeing, the rash young Asahel was determined to distinguish himself by slaying the mighty Abner. As the fleet young man gained in the pursuit, Abner sought to distract him to some other goal. But Asahel refused to turn aside, so Abner tried again, "Why should I slay you? I do not want to disgrace myself in the eyes of your family." When the foolish young man refused to be distracted from his purpose, the crafty and experienced old warrior suddenly turned and thrust him through with his spear.

In the arena of physical exploits, the advantage of strength lies with the young. To the middle-aged goes the advantage of skill and sometimes endurance. In the world of sports, the upper thirties or lower forties mark the end of career days. For most ordinary occupations, physical strength no longer determines performance. Nevertheless, the time comes when the aging of the body begins to take its toll. Beyond sixty, physical strength definitely diminishes. The suppleness of joints and quickness of movement decreases. Sometimes we face loss of sight or hearing. The frequency of chronic illness and the need for medication increase. Fatigue that does not go away may begin to beset us.

While much is being done by medical science and good health care to push these problems into later years, there is ultimately no way to escape them. Whether at the moment we are thinking of retirement, of staying out of the nursing home or of eventual length of life, we must face these physical realities. Our physical bodies, in which mind and spirit dwell, are set within certain limitations of time. The years beyond sixty-five, retirement time, should be the discretionary years—time to choose our activities according to strength, to continue intellectual adventures, to serve others with a new freedom or perhaps to travel. It is a time to reminisce, perhaps to write our memoirs—a legacy to our children and grandchildren.

Mind Outlasts Body

The good news is that in the area of intellect, there is no real evidence that continued mental capacities experience the certainty of decline which surrounds the physical body. To be sure, there are plenty of myths about aging and plenty of denigrating insinuations from the cult of youth worship. According to some, to be old is to be forgetful, to be forgetful is to be senile and when one is senile, life is over. The folk tales would have us believe that the elderly cannot learn new things, no more memorizing poetry or Bible verses. Older folks cannot keep up in table games requiring concentrated thought. What a myth! Most of the Scrabble players I know enough to shun are older than I am! They say you can't teach an old dog new tricks. I'm not so sure. Just maybe we "old dogs" have gotten smart enough to know we don't have to learn new tricks.

Research indicates some slowing of the intellectual processes. It takes a bit longer to do mathematical equations, to memorize either poetry or prose, to bring up from our memory-bank names, facts or ideas. But with a bit more time, the memory functions are intact. Barring any mental illness or physical diseases which affect nerve functions, the human mind will serve its possessor well for a hundred years or more.

However, people abuse their minds just as they abuse their bodies—by failing to exercise them. Many people do little or no challenging or thought-provoking reading. Simply to go to factory or office, doing assigned and routine tasks year after year, to come home to television and movies, to do no more creative thinking than to plan how to spend the weekend, certainly does not develop a disciplined mind with which to make fifteen or twenty years of retirement interesting and productive.

Still we must realize that mind and body are tied together. Eventually the decline of the body brings the mind with it. There will come an eventual weariness of living, a desire for release. In our time, we have good reason for saying, "Hurrah for old age." Physically and mentally, this generation of retirees has the prospect of more years of enjoyment and usefulness than any generation before us, but there is no fountain of youth.

Recently, I was touched by an article in Newsweek. Eli A. Rubinstein, in "The Not So Golden Years," describes his own experience of retirement and the prospects which he sees before him.[2]

Mr. Rubinstein speaks of having enjoyed a fulfilling career and of being in good health, financially secure and still active in community affairs. But he hates growing old, realizing "that it is all downhill from here." The residents who share the retirement facility with Eli Rubinstein are, by his own description, an elite group—proud of past achievements, fortunate in their present comfortable status, but missing the joys of past accomplishments. Twenty percent have serious physical ailments. He watches as one by one they are taken off to the hospital. The whole company plays a watching game—waiting for their own ship to hit that inevitable iceberg and sink.

Nothing, he concludes, takes the place of being young and vigorous with one's faculties still intact. And on a personal level, even getting up in the morning is a mixed blessing. Mr. Rubinstein defends his dismal view of old age by saying it teaches him to "seize the day." Enjoy what you have while you have it.

I agree that, from a purely physical and material viewpoint, these are the cold hard facts. However, I, want to say something more cheerful about old age. I would not want the medical scientists or the Lord Himself to think that we oldsters do not appreciate the years that have been added to our lives. By my own thesis, climbing down the ladder is harder than climbing up. But it is worth the climb. Beyond the inevitable facts of life and death lies the realm of the spirit. One's individual philosophy of life, one's personal religious faith, will determine the quality of those after-retirement years more than their physical circumstances.

3. Making Peace with Death

Jesus said to her, "I am the resurrection and the life. He who believes in me, though he may die, he shall live."

(John 11:25)

**The human body
always comes
with a
lifetime guarantee.**

When I was a young pastor, a popular religious song entitled "Death Is Only a Dream" was making its rounds. Occasionally, it would turn up at a funeral where I presided. My heart always bled a bit at that song. It did not fit my theology or my Bible knowledge at all. It had no place in Christian faith nor at anybody's funeral. "Who are these people trying to fool?" I would ask myself. Death is serious and sober business. Death is the enemy. In the patriarchal period of biblical history, we are told, death reigned and people were all their lifetime subject to bondage because of the fear of death. But Jesus broke the bondage.

Concepts of the Afterlife

In the Judeo-Christian tradition, death is much more than the demise of the physical body. As noted in the previous chapter, death is inevitable and death is final. The gates of death swing only in one direction. Once in the Old Testament, three times in the ministry of Jesus and twice for the Apostles those gates were reversed, but only temporarily. When Jesus by the power of the resurrection broke the grip of death, it was not to do away with physical dying but to add the dimension of eternal life, to guarantee that the spirit lives on beyond the grave and to say that what one does in this life, in response to the work of Jesus Christ, determines the quality of the life beyond this one.

Beyond the question of what one wants to do, or be, or achieve in life is the question of how one comes to the end of life in light of the realities of eternity. A part of living is to prepare for dying. This concern about the reality of the after-life and its quality is not something peculiar to the Christian religion. People throughout the ages—Mesopotamians, Egyptians, Greeks and Romans—had some notions of a life beyond this one. The Eastern religions with their concepts of reincarnation and a final arrival at Nirvana, or identification with the "world soul," also agree that physical death is not the end of existence. These notions, however, are not always related to the moral behavior of the individual in this present life. In light of this well nigh universal curiosity and concern about the nature of the afterlife, one ancient writer observed, "If there is not a conscious existence after this life, then there ought to be." With reference to the effects of moral behavior on the quality of the afterlife, one of the Greek philosophers is supposed to have said he does not know whether or not the gods will forgive men's sins, and even if they will, he does not know whether they ought to.

Biblical Assurance of Eternal Life

Not until the coming of Christianity and the clear teaching of the New Testament is the nature of the afterlife plainly articulated. The teaching of heaven for the righteous and hell for the wicked is sharply delineated. For the first time in religious history, the promise of heaven becomes an inducement to religious persuasion, a tool of evangelism. In Christianity first, forgiveness became a major theological foundation stone, a divine and human grace, the touchstone of personal salvation, to forgive and be forgiven. "For if ye forgive men their trespasses, your heavenly Father will also forgive you. But if you forgive not men their trespasses, neither will your Father forgive your trespasses" (Matthew 6:14-15).

Our Western civilization has been most largely influenced by the Christian concepts of the afterlife. This still does not mean that everyone heeds the biblical injunction to seek forgiveness of sin and make peace with God. Most people, however, do give some serious thought to the meaning of life and the nature of its end. There are many—too many—who try to satisfy themselves with lofty philosophical concepts of the interrelation of all of creation (including human life) or of the continuation of life in the memories of their friends or the ongoing lives of their children and grandchildren.

There are those who, because of their devotion to science, cannot accept anything which demands belief in the supernatural, and Christianity most certainly does. Such individuals are likely to opt for a simple atheism, a materialistic world view. A brash young man once said to me, "People ought to know that when they are dead, the worms get them, and that is the end." Job was well aware of what the worms do to the natural body, but he was quite confident that in his flesh he would see God (Job 19:26).

Others have chosen to believe some form of Eastern religion which promises an absorption into a world soul where the individual is forgotten. I was intrigued in reading recently of the death of an elderly movie star who had once been the darling and idol of vast audiences, and whose words about life and death many would regard seriously. She was reported to have said shortly before her death, "I do not fear hell, and I do not anticipate heaven. I am looking forward to oblivion."

The Christian invitation to eternal life through Jesus Christ contrasts happily with these gloomy thoughts of oblivion. Although we usually think of our initial salvation experience in terms of dealing with the guilt of sin, of being born again into a new life of forgiveness and peace; salvation, in reality, also provides a first step into an understanding of the meaning of life. This step sets the goals and parameters of life, pointing to a time when the earthly journey, with its joys and sorrows, achievements and disappointments, is exchanged with confidence for a new life that is eternal. Though not always articulated, this underlying consciousness of death presses the urgency of first finding forgiveness of sin and peace with God to whom all must answer in the Judgment Day. What one takes to that meeting with Creator, Redeemer and Judge must all be settled prior to the time of physical death. "It is appointed for men to die once, but after this the judgment" (Hebrews 9:27).

The Christian gospel urges upon everyone the importance of making peace with God early in life. Death is the great unknown, coming to young as well as old. I am most concerned with addressing the elderly and impressing on each of us the importance of having the issue of eternal destiny settled as a way to face confidently the years of retirement and physical decline.

Peace with God

Under the concept of "becoming a Christian" or "making peace with God," we commonly think of having our sins forgiven, of being restored to a right relation with God, so that we no longer fear death, the judgment and the thought of punishment or hell. In my own mind, there are other benefits and experiences which follow as a consequence of our making peace with God. The next step is what I would call "making peace with the world." It simply means learning to live in, to accept, a world that is not what its Creator intended when He first made it. It has been spoiled by sin—physically, relationally and spiritually.

Peace with the World

In this life a person's lot is labor, weariness, boredom and often disappointment. It is a place where things do not always turn out fairly; not just mildly disappointing but often with crushing tragedy. And these things happen impartially to Christian and non-Christian alike. In fact, it often seems that the wicked enjoy a life of prosperity and ease, while those who profess godliness suffer temptation, trial and disappointment. However, those biblical writers who inquire most deeply into this seeming inequity have concluded that the final payoff is not to be expected in this life. There is a day of reckoning for the wicked and of recompense for the righteous. The Psalmist David observed, "But as for me, my feet had almost stumbled, my steps had nearly slipped, for I was envious of the boastful, when I saw the prosperity of the wicked...until I went into the sanctuary of God; then I understood their end. Surely you set them in slippery places: you cast them down to destruction" (Psalm 73:2,3,17,18).

In the realm of natural phenomena, things operate by what we call natural law. If a child falls into the water, it drowns whether the parents are Christian or non-Christian. When a tornado roars through town, the houses of the righteous and the wicked alike are destroyed. When a deadly disease stalks the land, germs or viruses ask no questions about the morality of the victims whom they attack. It is this relentless impartiality of natural law which is difficult for many people to reconcile with the providence of God, most of all, the notion of a loving God.

Peace with One's Self

A third aspect of this salvation orientation is the matter of making peace with one's self. In spite of the devastation people sometimes experience from the grudges which they carry, generally the most difficult area of forgiveness is simply the problem of forgiving one's self. Many persons who claim to believe that God has promised to forgive their sin upon confession still do not find peace because they are not able to forgive themselves. Both personal and pastoral experience has made me acutely aware of this problem.

Some years ago at one of our local community evangelistic campaigns, I was asked to be in charge of the counseling room. It was my responsibility to see that persons who came for counsel were assigned to a competent and compatible worker who would hear their confession and help in dealing with their need.

One evening when the invitation was given, a very mature gentleman came for help. I asked one of our more experienced pastors to sit with him. Much later when most of the counselors and their counselees had left the room, I noticed that these two were still in conversation. The minister beckoned for me to come, so I went over and sat with them. The minister explained, "We have gone over all that the Bible says about the way of salvation, but Brother John does not seem able to find peace. Can you help us?" I wondered what I might say that the older minister had not already explained, but I tried, beginning to inquire gently into the man's problem.

"Do you feel that you understand what the Bible teaches about the way of salvation, the way to peace with God?"

"Yes."

"Do you believe that God will fulfill His promise to forgive those who come to Him in true repentance?"

"Oh, yes."

"Are you sincere and open in your request for forgiveness? You are not holding back anything you are unwilling to confess?"

"Nothing that I know."

"Would you, by any chance, be holding a grudge against someone?"

"None."

I was running out of probes. On a sudden impulse, surely at the prompting of the Holy Spirit, I said, "Have you forgiven yourself?"

He looked at me sharply, in an almost startled way. Then I saw a light come into his eye, and he said quietly, "Maybe I haven't." We talked a bit longer, prayed together and the brother went on his way in peace, which I have every reason to believe he enjoyed the rest of his days on earth.

Zest for Living

I have spoken earnestly about the importance of making peace with God and of being ready to die; that is, to make the transition from the physical world to the realms of the Spirit without fear, perhaps even with a measure of anticipation. But I want to be very clear, a vast difference exists between being ready to die in the sense of being unafraid of its consequences and being ready to die in the sense of having relinquished all interest in the natural world.

Henry was a college student who began attending the church where I was pastor. To save money, he had a room off campus and made his own meals. Henry developed a strangulated hernia. He put off going to the doctor as long as he could bear the pain, which was too long. When he finally had surgery, gangrene had set in and medical procedures were futile. Henry's parents came from another state to be with him. His father, being concerned about his son's spiritual welfare, shared with Henry the seriousness of his condition and asked, "Henry, are you ready to die?" The son's reply was, "Father, I am not afraid to die, but I am not ready to die."

The answer did not entirely satisfy the father, and he shared his anxiety with me. What I told the father I also shared with family and friends a few days later at Henry's funeral. Referring to Henry's response, I assured the congregation that I believed his attitude to be exactly right for a young man. Being a Christian can take away the fear of death, but it should not take away the zest for physical life, nor dim the anticipation of joys to be savored, nor steal the ambition for a life of worthwhile achievement.

In youth we put the thought of death far away. Though we acknowledge death, it belongs with old age. It is something that won't happen to us, at least not now. There are too many things to be done and to enjoy. In remembering my own youthful musings about death, I thought in terms of those things I would miss if I should die now. I wanted to get married and have a family. I wanted to have a big farm. (I never did get a farm!) I wanted to travel. I wanted to make some money. Death would thwart all of these, so I put the thought far away.

When I was quite small, there was a tragedy in a family of my parents' acquaintance. A small daughter of perhaps six or eight years somehow caught her clothing on fire at the heating stove and was burned so that she died almost immediately. The time was mid-December. Hearing that account as a child, I remember that my first thought was, "What a terrible thing— to die just before Christmas, to miss all the anticipated excitement."

A more mature Bible knowledge has assured me that in God's provision for the afterlife, no one, whether they die in youth or old age, will spend any part of eternity regretting the things they "missed" because their life on earth was cut short. Eternity will be filled with good things which surpass, make up for and leave behind any of those things we once imagined as necessary to a complete and happy earthly experience.

Death, the Intruder
You may be expecting me to say that making peace with death is an accomplishment of maturity, a part of growing old. While that idea may hold a measure of truth, making peace with death is basically an outgrowth of Christian faith, a making peace with all of life, including death. It is seeing one's self in full perspective, in light of eternity as well as time. Again, this is the first step toward getting down off the ladder of personal ambition, self-adulation and self-importance onto the firm ground of human wholeness, of grasping our body and spirit existence, of being at home in both the physical and spiritual realm. The problem, as Paul explains in II Corinthians 5:6, lies in the fact that while we are at home in the body, we are absent from the Lord. The things of the flesh, the material interests, tend to dim or crowd out the realities of the spirit world. Of all God's creation, only humankind has the capacity of life in both the physical and the spiritual world. Herein is our great glory and our dilemma.

Once again, I believe that God intends for all of us to enjoy life and to cherish it, whether we are young or old. When I say "enjoy life," I mean it, even in face of the fact that millions of people in the world live in poverty, in circumstances most undesirable, even in danger of starvation. It is amazing that even in such circumstances, people cherish life and manage to draw some small joys and satisfactions from it. In almost every culture (with a few oddball philosophies excepted), suicide has been looked upon as abnormal, an affront against God and human personality.

When I say that God intends happiness for the human race, I come from the theological understanding that the inequities of human existence, the differences between rich and poor and the differences between the oppressed and the oppressor, even the seeming fickleness of natural disasters—famine, fire and flood—are not to be thought of as the will of God. They have come about because of the intrusion of sin, an intrusion in which humankind was the willing cooperator. These are now the circumstances within which God Himself must operate. In Jesus Christ, God has made wonderful provisions. First, for our restoration to God in peace and, second, in giving us a basis for understanding and accepting those unequal circumstances, good fortune or tragedy, which fall into every life.

If you like those little riddles or jokes which depend on a play on words, try this one from the Bible: "What Bible character learned to talk younger than anyone else on record?" The answer is Job; he cursed the day he was born! Well, not exactly. But Job, in the midst of his unexplained and seemingly unfair tribulations, became weary of life to the point of wishing he had never been born. That particular pit of despair has doubtless been shared by many, many individuals, at least for a time. On the other hand, Job was a most persistent character. He demanded an audience with God and an explanation of what seemed to him to be unfair and arbitrary action on the part of God. Job finally had his day in court with God.

While his questions may not have been answered exactly in the form of Job's demands, he learned that God was acting entirely within His sovereign rights, not arbitrarily, and that His love toward His children was steadfast and abiding.

From Generation to Generation

How then does one make peace with death? Earlier I suggested a certain natural wisdom comes with aging. God has established a patterned life process—birth, childhood, youth, adulthood, old age and death. Though it is normal to struggle against the process of aging, no one can be unaware of it nor deny its rightness. It is easy to acknowledge a certain beauty and grandeur to the historical process of passing the torch from generation to generation. We receive inspiration and challenge from our parents. We make our contribution to the work and wisdom of community and culture. Hopefully, we pass on to our children a better world than the one we inherited. That is a worthy ideal. Yet when we realize this process involves our personal physical death, we are likely to draw back.

The physical time clock which ticks away in our bodies does give us some help. There comes a time when our physical strength diminishes. We tire more easily and sight and hearing may diminish to the point of being troublesome. Physical illnesses of sundry kinds are more common. Like it or not, we become dependent on the medicine bottle. Even the zest for food may diminish, and our favorite dishes may not taste like they once did. If we are fortunate, we may have enjoyed some of the things which in youth we thought were indispensable to life. We may have achieved some of the goals we set for ourselves. Now the "worlds to conquer" no longer beckon us with the urgency and glamour they once possessed.

A frank realization and understanding of these things can

be helpful. Death does not seem quite so strange and forbidding. A few years ago when my siblings and I had all arrived safely in our seventies, I had the courage to say to them, "Well, when the time comes that the doctor tells us we have a condition that is terminal, we dare not think of it as a tragedy. We have each had a good and fair share of life."

People who experience severe illness almost to the point of death often report that the things which they considered important in this life fade into relative insignificance. Their value appraisal of material things had somehow been over-estimated. In fact, I can verify this by personal experience.

Some years ago a gallstone blockage developed into a life-threatening case of pancreatitis for me, so severe that the surgeon delayed operating for a day or two to see if I could be stabilized. I didn't know how sick I really was. I had no fear of dying, and my plans were only for getting well again. Yet after the ordeal of pain, the oblivion of surgery and the restriction of living for a week at the end of an array of tubes and needles, I discovered a strange detachment from the ordinary things of life. They had lost their importance. But I did recover. I got back into the stream of daily life and responsibility, and the feeling of detachment disappeared.

Putting Death in Its Place

Even for older people, who have reassured themselves of their peace with God and acceptance of His will and providence in their lives and who have acquired a measure of the natural wisdom of life, even for them there is a difference between being reconciled to dying and being tired of living. I do not encourage the "tired of living" attitude for anyone, though they have lived to be ninety or a hundred. I am sure God is not surprised at the way in which even the very old, though they may be in painful and restricted circumstances, still cling to life. Best known for his lying, the devil was very near the truth when he said, "Skin for skin! yes, all that a man has will he give for his life" (Job 2:4).

Samuel Gerber, in his book *Learning to Die*, suggests, "Our struggle against death is simply an indication of the fact that deep down we know that originally God did not create us for death. Death is and remains unnatural—something irrational. Consequently, every fiber of our being protests against the clutching hand of the grim reaper that is stretched out to get us."[1]

The concept that physical death was not in God's original plan is important. Recently someone suggested to me that the experience of Enoch—"And Enoch walked with God: and he was not, for God took him" (Genesis 5:24)—may have been God's original intention. We can only wonder about that.

In Old Testament times, people had little relief from the gloom of death. Though a number of Old Testament writers testify to their belief in life beyond the grave, the revelation is incomplete and the gloom only lightly relieved.

With the coming of Jesus, the picture changes dramatically. Jesus' own clash with death, His victory in the resurrection, released humankind from bondage. Both sin and death were overcome, and we were set free. Jesus' very casual references to physical death always puzzled His disciples. (They still puzzle His followers.) The barrier between the physical and spiritual worlds seemed all but nonexistent in His thinking. When called to the bedside of the ailing Lazarus, He was not perturbed but continued about His business. First, Jesus informed the disciples that Lazarus' sickness was not unto death but for the glory of God. Then after two days, he declared that Lazarus was sleeping, and He would go awaken him. To paraphrase, the disciples response was, "That's great, if he is sleeping, then he will get well." Finally, in recognition of the disciples' limitations, Jesus said plainly, "Lazarus is dead." He further told them He was glad He had not been there (to restore Lazarus from illness) because He was about to do something more wonderful, something to help them believe— believe in His own power over death. Even though the disciples witnessed the raising of Lazarus, it is certain they really did not comprehend the magnitude of Jesus' action until after His own resurrection, and perhaps they did not fully comprehend it even then. So it is with us. We believe that Jesus takes away the sting of death and the victory of the grave, yet, in our humanity, we find it difficult to apply to the experience of our own dying.

Welcome Death!

Finally, there comes a time when it is entirely proper for us to long for our home-going, for release from all earthly limitations and distresses and to enter into the presence of Christ and the experience of the eternal. In my years as a pastor, I have been happy for those persons I visited and counseled who, although facing terminal illness and knowing that their time on earth was short, could speak openly and frankly about it and say that it was all right. Certainly, they had their struggles, common to human experience, had gone through the stages of shock, anger, bargaining with God and finally of acceptance. Many times there was also a final twinge of concern for their family and regret at leaving their loved ones. But a definitive sense of peace and acceptance reigned— they could say they were ready to go, they were not afraid and they were grateful to their Lord who had given them fruitful years, the assurance of forgiveness and eternal life.

Sometimes there is a real longing for death, often expressed in terms of "going home," a desire to be freed from bodily pain and suffering, a desire to be with the Lord. I remember my Great-Uncle Johnny Wenger. I visited him a number of times in his last illness. I don't know that he was in any great pain, but he was weary. He had no close family and any responsibility was a burden. He was ready to go home. On several occasions he said to me, "I just don't know why Jesus doesn't come and take me home." There is a time at which death ceases to be the enemy and becomes a welcome friend.

4. The Problem of Illness

This sickness is not unto death but for the glory of God.

(John 11:4b)

Upon being asked about his health, Grandpa replied, "Well, I'm better than I was but not as good as I used to be before I got as bad as I am now."

Having spent a chapter on the problem of being reconciled to the reality of death, perhaps the questions of human illness and physical affliction have been covered. Not quite. It is true that illness and affliction always carry with them the specter of death. To deal with one is in some measure to deal with the other. Yet in all the years since being driven from the Garden of Eden, humanity has puzzled over the problem of living with bodily affliction. From whence does this monster come? How are its victims selected? And how do we reconcile its presence with the providence of God? Particularly when, as in Christianity, we want to believe that God is a loving God. In a broader sense, the problem of dealing with the natural evil which befalls us (illness, affliction, fire, flood, earthquake and accident) has been the medium of turning people to understanding faith, or turning them away from faith, more often than any other single issue.

Pain, the Constant Companion

Bodily affliction is no respecter of age. From the cradle to the moment of death, our bodies are subject to pain and malfunction. It does become one of the problems which must be dealt with more specifically as we grow older. With advancing years, the non-life-threatening illnesses and limitations become more frequent. Pain becomes a more constant companion. Trips to the doctor's office occupy too much of our travel time, and the medicine shelf becomes larger and larger.

When I was young, most respectable older people, it seemed, at least had rheumatism and spent the winter months huddled by the fireside. Even with the good news for the present generation of aging persons—longer life expectancy, better health care, more years of productive activity—most older adults still have plenty of time to ponder the source, the reason and the purpose of bodily affliction and decline.

Jesus spent much of His time in a healing ministry. Once word got around that a healer with great power walked the land, Jesus was simply overwhelmed. His response was most touching, and the teaching which accompanied it quite instructive. Jesus declared that he had come to preach repentance and to announce the coming of the Kingdom. It seems the constant pressure of the crowds imploring His healing power should have interfered with His mission.

The loving Saviour never turned away those who came to Him. Sometimes He asked them to keep it quiet, to tell no one what had happened. However, Jesus' power to deal with the old, old problem of suffering was so striking that those who were healed proclaimed it abroad wherever they went. We have no idea how many people Jesus healed. The Gospel writers observe frequently that He "healed many" and on at least two occasions that "He healed them all" (Matthew 8:16; 12:15). The Gospels also detail a number of Jesus' healings apparently for the purpose of giving specific theological teaching on the presence and purpose of sickness and affliction in human experience.

There was some requirement of faith, on the part of those who came, before Jesus could minister the healing miracle. This requirement is not always clear in the Gospel accounts; sometimes it is specifically mentioned and other times implied. In His own home community, Jesus encountered marked unbelief so that the writer observes, "Now He could do no mighty work there except that He laid His hands on a few sick people and healed them" (Mark 6:5). Another time Jesus said, "According to your faith let it be done to you" (Matthew 9:29).

The Source of Illness

A common notion in Jesus' day held that sickness and affliction were direct judgments of God on human sin. As a matter of fact, that notion has been prevalent throughout much of human history. Job's three friends insisted mightily that Job's affliction was the result of sin—unacknowledged, hidden or even unrecognized —and it took the direct intervention of God to get them off his back. The same notion is very common in our own day and is easily latched onto by persons whose guilty consciences give them some reason to believe they deserve to suffer. As I grew up, I was acquainted with a neighboring family who had a severely retarded child. The mother confided to my mother that she was sure this child had been sent to her as punishment for the wicked ways of her youth.

Once when Jesus healed a man who had been born blind (John 9), the disciples asked Jesus directly, "Who sinned, this man or his parents, that he was born blind?" Jesus' answer shattered a lot of people's pet theology, "Neither this man nor his parents sinned, but that the works of God should be revealed in him." This is a double-barreled answer. First of all, Jesus explicitly says there is no direct link between personal affliction and personal sin. Neither birth defects, crippling affliction, nor common illnesses are signs or evidence of moral delinquency.

He further asserted the man had been born blind that the work of God might be made manifest. Can our human afflictions be for the glory of God? Does He set up these situations arbitrarily just to get attention focused on Himself? Before I try to answer, let me bring in another illustration.

In Mark 2 we encounter the paralytic who was brought by four friends to Jesus for healing. The house was so packed there was no way to carry him in on a stretcher. The resourceful quartet removed some of the roofing tiles and let the man down directly in front of Jesus. Seeing their faith, Jesus did a very unexpected thing. He said to the man, "Your sins are forgiven." While that was obviously not what the man wanted, Jesus got the desired result. The scribes standing by immediately went into a tizzy. "Who can forgive sins but God alone?" (In that, of course, they were exactly right.) So while Jesus had them off balance, He pushed them completely over. "Which is easier, to say to the paralytic, 'Your sins are forgiven you,' or to say, 'Arise, take up your bed and walk?'" Jesus proceeded to demonstrate His authority to forgive sin by healing the paralytic.

What Jesus did here has far-reaching implications for our understanding of the working of affliction and suffering in human experience. Jesus said or implied that sickness is the direct result of sin in the world, not personal guilt, but sin in the race! The consequences of sin in the race fall upon individuals rather indiscriminately. Jesus also said or implied that dealing with sin as manifest in human suffering requires divine power. In this sense suffering may be for the glory of God.

Now don't be frightened. I'm not going where you might think! Throughout the world's history, illness and affliction have been dealt with in several ways. Sometimes direct divine intervention occurred. For three glorious years, Jesus turned the medical (and the theological) world on its head, healing people contrary to all natural expectation by the dozens and perhaps hundreds. The apostles kept up some semblance of this healing ministry during their lifetimes, after which the expectations concerning healing seem to have gone back to normal. The church, however, has kept alive for two thousand years some anticipation and teaching of divine healing.

The principal way God provides physical healing comes through the knowledge of science and medicine, which He has given human beings to discover. I do not hesitate to say that the doctor or nurse who cares for me in illness is a minister of God to me for healing, whether or not she or he is a Christian. In my estimation, however, it is so much better if my doctor or nurse is a Christian, allowing us to work together more happily and effectively and with better understanding of the spiritual and scientific dimensions of healing.

Understanding and Misunderstanding

In the history of the Christian church, the notions about healing have run to both ends of the spectrum. At one extreme is the notion that we live completely by natural law; sickness and affliction come by the invasion of germs or by gene deficiency. Salvation has to do only with the soul, and God is not particularly concerned about what happens to the body.

On the other hand, one encounters the teaching that physical healing is part of salvation; that it is not God's will for any Christian to be sick, and if such is the case, there must be a lack of faith or a lack of understanding or both.

The teaching that physical healing is a part of the atonement made when Jesus suffered and died usually begins with a citation of Isaiah 53:4-5 where the older terms "griefs and sorrows" are sometimes rendered "sicknesses and pains" and where "with His stripes we are healed" becomes a reference to physical healing. This idea of healing has both a yes and a no abiding in it. Having said as I did that sickness is the result of sin in the race, it follows that divine power is required to deal with it. Jesus, by his death and resurrection, broke the power of sin (bringing salvation) and death (doing away with sickness and dying). We receive salvation immediately upon accepting Jesus as Saviour. However, Jesus did not remove sickness and dying from natural life.

I have heard it said that death is the ultimate healer. There is truth in this expression. The believer carries nothing of pain, death or tears into glory. But the notion that we should be able in this life to heal sickness and disability with a simple word of faith is a misinterpretation of biblical teaching. In fact, I consider this one of the most cruel distortions of truth which well-meaning Christians have ever imposed upon themselves or others. To tell persons already struggling with the mysteries of God's providence that if only they had enough faith, they would be healed is to lay upon them a cruel blow, a hopeless and misguided load of guilt. This approach has more than once been the undoing, rather than the establishment, of someone's peace.

Biblical Teaching on Healing

What then does the Bible teach regarding the believer's recourse in times of bodily affliction? Both the Old and New Testaments include numerous instances where family or friends prayed earnestly for the healing of those who were ill. Sometimes the answer was yes, sometimes no. As with all other sincere prayers, we have the assurance that God hears and ministers His grace, but the Bible provides no discernible pattern to suggest the answer will always be in the physical form which the petitioner may have in mind.

The Bible does give clear indication that God cares about both the spiritual and physical well-being of His children. Numerous scriptures encourage us to pray for ourselves and for one another for both physical and spiritual wholeness. James 5 gives particular instruction for a physical healing ministry of the church which we call anointing with oil. This provision has all the marks of a religious ordinance—a visible symbol (oil), the dedication of prayer and the ministry of the church by an appointed representative (elder). Note the three main considerations—believing prayer, cleansing of sin and the healing of the body. It is not, however, a universal ordinance commanded upon all believers. Instead, it is a discretionary provision for those who want to call upon God in this way. It should not be confused with the sacrament of extreme unction as a preparation for imminent death. Nor is it a magic formula by which we can twist God's arm to make Him comply with our human desires. It is rather a faith commitment, placing ourselves and a loved one into God's wise and caring providence.

As a pastor and bishop, I have been called many times to provide this ministry, in the name of the church, to those who were sick. While it did not always result in physical healing, it was always a satisfying ministry. To illustrate the breadth of its coverage, I share a few examples.

The pastor of one of our congregations asked me as bishop to go with him to perform an anointing service. The woman requesting the anointing was in a Petersburg, West Virginia, hospital. I do not remember the medical name of her particular ailment, but she suffered from a severe blood condition which included the danger that clotting might at any time block her arteries causing death. She had been warned not to let her feet dangle over the edge of the bed or chair, or to do anything else which might in the slightest way restrict the flow of blood in her limbs. The doctor had ordered tests every few hours to monitor her condition.

We ministered to her the message of James 5, talked of her faith and commitment to God, her reason and desire for physical healing. Finally, we performed the anointing service and ended with a period of believing prayer committing all to the Lord. The pastor and I went on our way.

Shortly afterward the nurse came to take blood for the periodic check. In the laboratory she ran the test and to her amazement, the blood reading was normal. Believing she had muffed the procedure, she returned to the patient for another blood sample and ran the test again. Again, the reading was normal. The puzzled nurse went back to the patient's room to consider the situation. Just then the doctor came in. After telling the doctor of the situation, the nurse suggested they do the test once more with the doctor supervising the procedure. Together they ran the test. The results were still normal.

The woman continued to heal and was soon dismissed from the hospital. She later moved from the community and I lost track of her, but I know that for many years afterward she lived a normal life.

I was also called upon one night on behalf of a woman in the Harrisonburg, Virginia, hospital who was requesting anointing. I called her pastor and together we ministered to her. In the course of our conversation, it became clear her mind was set on physical healing and returning to normal life. She confidently expected it. Following the anointing and for several days, she seemed to be making steady improvement. I visited her again some days later when the pastor also happened to be present. I discovered a subtle change, not so much physical to my untrained eye, but a change in attitude. She spoke of "going home" in a way that I clearly understood to refer to the heavenly home. She expressed her readiness to go. As we left the room, I said to the pastor, "She is not going to get well; she has changed her mind." Several days later I was in charge of her funeral.

This particular instance has a very interesting sequel. Some twenty years later, my wife and I were attending a viewing for a longtime friend in another community. A woman whom I did not recognize came to us and called me by name. "You probably don't know me," she remarked, "but you preached at my mother's funeral." As she identified herself, it all came back to me.

"Perhaps," I suggested, "I can tell you more about your mother that you may not know. I also had an anointing service for her before she died."

"Yes, I do know," was her response. "I was the one who called you the night of her anointing."

I told her of my perception of her mother changing her mind about physical healing. "Yes," she responded, "I know about that too. It was a remarkable experience."

Another time I was called to the bedside of a young man. I had been both pastor and personal friend to Leonard. He was dying of leukemia, leaving a wife and three young daughters. His wife was understandably distraught. Leonard gave me no indication of being interested, but, as a gesture to his wife's concern, we broke the usual rule of waiting for the individual to ask and suggested an anointing service. To this he readily agreed. However, he was too ill to take any real part or display any great interest in the preliminary discussion. There was no manifest evidence of any physical improvement resulting from the anointing. The benefit, as I observed, was primarily to his wife. She—having used every available means, medical and spiritual, and having through the religious service committed her husband, herself and her situation to the Lord—was able to accept her husband's death a short time later with a much larger measure of grace and peace.

Grandma Bowers had lived a long and useful life, working hard and unselfishly to serve her family and neighbors. She spent her last days living with a daughter and son-in-law. In her last illness, she called for anointing. I took Dr. Charles Hertzler, then resident in the community where I was pastor, with me. On the way to the house, Dr. Charlie let me know of his misgivings. "What are you trying to do? Keep this poor old lady alive who has already lived out her years and has very little capacity left for useful or enjoyable living?"

"Well," I said, "as a doctor, you know that people have a way of clinging to life. Besides, I feel there is more to this than a demand for extended years."

At the house we talked with Grandma about the meaning of James 5, about a good conscience, the Lord's providential care and direction of life and, finally, about the home He has prepared in glory. We did the anointing ceremony and closed with prayer, leaving Grandma quiet and satisfied. On the way home, Dr. Charlie remarked thoughtfully, "Now I understand what you are doing. I'm in favor of it."

When my own turn in the hospital came, facing surgery and knowing that my condition was life-threatening, I thought of all the anointing services I had ministered to others. While I was not particularly disturbed about the possibility of dying and did not feel I had any great reason for imploring the Lord to extend my years, it just seemed the right thing to do. So, with my own pastor and a little group of family and friends about me, the ordinance of anointing was ministered to me. When friends and family were gone and the nurse had prepared me for the night, I felt a gentle peace and confidence.

Obviously, I recovered. So who gets the credit? Without hesitation I give the credit to God Himself, and that detracts nothing from my recognition of the skills of the doctors and nurses who took care of me or my gratitude to them for their competent and kindly care. As indicated earlier, I believe the advances in medical science, which God has given us to discover, are His gift of healing to us. They do in some measure alleviate, but do not eradicate, the physical ravages of sin in the race. The blessings of longer years, better personal health, more opportunity for a life of enjoyment and service and more knowledge of proper diet are in reality the gift of God to this generation of older adults.

No conflict of interest exists between making full use of medical science and, at the same time, exercising the special ministry of anointing as a symbol of the divine interest in, and provision for, the physical well-being of God's people. Those who have been strong on faith healing have not always kept this in biblical perspective. Some have taught that calling on the services of medical science denies faith in God and is a barrier to His ministry of divine healing. I cannot agree. I have personally known some very tragic consequences for people who discontinued the use of medicine in favor of "just trusting God."

Illness as God's Problem

We have struggled with the problems of sickness, misfortune and, finally, death since the expulsion of our first parents from the Garden of Eden. The question demands attention. Perhaps we should try looking at it from God's point of view. God created us for good, for a life of purpose and joy on earth which we cannot now describe because it has never been realized in history. Instead came the experience of our disobedience. God's plan was thwarted. By sin Adam and Eve brought upon themselves death—the spiritual death of separation from God, physical death with all its antecedent woes, not only on human life but on the rest of creation as well.

This is the situation with which God must work. Within it He provides first for our salvation—a restoration to God in fellowship and eventually restoration of the created universe. Meanwhile, God works with us while we live in the physical world which includes sicknesses and calamities of all sorts. To the human eye and understanding, it appears that things operate according to natural law, and these laws appear quite inflexible. Sometimes we Christians may prefer to call this God's law, which is fine, except that we should remember the situation is not the way God intended it from the beginning.

Some time ago on a radio broadcast I heard something which proved a milestone in my own thinking about the problem of illness. A family who had early dedicated themselves to the work of mission was being interviewed. They went to school and prepared themselves for their chosen field of service. Shortly before they launched their career, the husband was stricken with a crippling malady. In the months that followed, other tragedies struck their family, bringing them to the depths both physically and emotionally.

With dreams shattered, they began slowly to rebuild. Eventually, with time and courage they were able to build a ministry suitable to the husband's limitations and become a blessing to many.

The interviewer asked the husband, "What did you think

during those months of pain and disappointment? What did you say to God? Did you accuse Him for His unfairness?"

There was a long pause. Then the husband replied, "I can truthfully say that I never thought of God as being unfair. I know that life is unfair, but it never occurred to me to think that God is unfair."

Therein lies a fine, but important, difference. Life is unfair. In this world of natural law, of cause and effect, no one is immune to the fates which, indeed, are grossly unfair. But Christian faith, the Christian relationship to God, says with assurance that God is not unfair.

Christianity has always had a strong sense of God's sovereignty, and we tend to ascribe all things good or bad to the will of God. In times of death or other pain, we may seek to console one another by saying, "It was God's will; He knows best." More and more, I have become careful of saying in such situations, "It was God's will." Things in our world are not the way God intended them. At best we can only think of these things as being God's will in a secondary sense. He works within a universe spoiled by sin. For us, it is a case of understanding Hebrews 2:8b, "But now we do not yet see all things put under Him."

Some years ago I compiled a minister's manual giving suggested formulas for a variety of religious ceremonies. I tried very hard to find words which would be correct, comforting and encouraging for funeral occasions. It wasn't easy. At such times we often hear the expression, "It pleased God in His wise providence to take out of the world..." I may not have improved much on the impressions likely to be evoked by these words, but I suggested the following replacement for funeral and burial occasions, "Now that our Heavenly Father in His wise and loving providence has called home to Himself..." The idea that it "pleased" God to inflict illness or cause death has been a stumbling block to many people and especially difficult for children to comprehend.

At such times it is necessary somehow to preserve the sovereignty of God—to be assured in our own minds that neither history nor our own personal affairs are beyond God's control. At the same time, we must understand that God is working within a situation which He did not will—a world deliberately chosen by humans through their own sin.

I recall one occasion of ministering to a family where an aged mother had just died. An otherwise very mature woman was crying hysterically, "I just can't believe in a God who would take away my dear mother." I don't recall that I even tried to restore her faith, but I did ponder the fact that the mother had lived for 88 years. By all accounts she had lived a good life and was no longer able to do the things that had made life meaningful for her. She would have needed constant care, and I am not sure the hysterical daughter would have wanted to provide such care for another five or ten years.

Just suppose for the moment we put all the responsibility on God for choosing the moment of birth and death for every individual. In the case of the 88-year-old mother, we may believe He chose wisely. Even so I don't think we may assume the particular details were God's "will" from the beginning. We may only say they were God's providential will for the given situation.

Perhaps I should say frankly that I believe in both the sovereignty and providence of God and in the operation of natural law. I would never say that it "pleases" God to put upon us affliction or determine our death. Yet I believe that God works within the situation for our good, our maturity and His glory. Job could not understand God's way of dealing with him, but he could say with confidence, "When He has tested me, I shall come forth as gold" (Job 23:10). I recognize the long tradition in both biblical and church history of referring to human fortune and misfortune as the "will of God." Perhaps, after all, in my attempt to enlighten our understanding and acceptance of the human situation, I cannot much improve upon the words we use.

The Mature Outlook

I am not saying that older people should learn to like illness. Just that as we age, we are likely to have more acquaintance with illness and more reason to ask ourselves how we might come to terms with it. As with many other things, the exuberance of youth and the business of middle age incline us to push it aside. In the soberness of older years, we will likely be obliged to make settlement. So how do I face the presence of sickness and infirmity?

First, Christian faith and philosophy allow me to understand that illness is part of the human condition, not some strange misfortune visited upon me unfairly. We all know individuals who complain constantly and bitterly about every ache and pain, making the most sunny day gloomy for themselves and those about them. On the other hand, there are those who bear pain with a contagious cheerfulness. The ancient Greeks, though not Christian, had a pattern of consoling each other with the assurance that there were always others who suffered disappointments and sorrows greater than their own.

Second, I take advantage of the medical understandings and treatments available to me. We are fortunate in our time to be the recipients of the advances medical science achieved during the past fifty years—heart and brain surgery, joint replacements, antibiotics and cancer cures. By the standards of even twenty-five years ago, many of us should be dead.

Third, I take care of my own health. Along with astounding discoveries in medicine and surgery, we have access to healthful dietary and exercise habits. No longer can there be any question about the harmful effects of tobacco, alcohol and other drugs. Regardless of the newly revived popularity of social drinking, we are well advised to stay clean and free. Vitamins and supplements have their place. They can be beneficial to most older persons, but they should be used wisely, on the advice or at least with the knowledge of a doctor. Exercise has long been held in esteem. Recent controlled studies have also demonstrated the superior benefits of aerobic exercise, in contrast to just plain hard work. By aerobic exercise, we mean rhythmic, sustained exercise which gets circulation going to a kind of health building rate which we learn to sense in our own bodies. There are many indoor and outdoor exercising devices from which to choose.

Most amazing is the way in which simple walking, in contrast to the jogging craze of a few years ago, has moved to the forefront among health builders. A mile or two, three or four times a week, at a pace suitable to one's own physical condition provides surprising benefits even into advanced years. An old health adage maintains, "An apple a day keeps the doctor away." Someone smartly added, "An onion a day keeps everybody away." Perhaps we may amend it again by saying, "A walk each day keeps nobody away—it makes you good company."

I will refrain from expanding on the subject of nutrition. Plenty of books, pamphlets and articles have been written about nutrition. It is good news that medical science now recognizes its importance in health care. Additional good news may be found in the fact that the information is not a medical secret, but is open to all. Matters of diet and nutrition lie largely in our own hands. We may eat vegetables, fruit and fiber and keep sugar, salt and fat in their place. North American eating habits from the good old Pennsylvania Dutch to the crossroads fast-food joints have notoriously cultivated our taste for sugar, salt and fat, and they are skillfully hidden in many tasty products. Older adults need a balanced diet just as much as children do. We also need to be careful to eat neither too much nor too little.

A fourth element of personal health and a powerful antidote to disease is simply a good and positive attitude toward life—the cultivation of a cheerful spirit. Solomon long ago proclaimed, "A merry heart does good like medicine" (Proverbs 17:22). Medical science took a long time before really putting this idea to a test. Doctors generally observe that those patients who persistently keep a positive, hopeful and cheerful attitude stand a much better chance of recovery from either illness or surgery, often achieving it faster, than those who are fearful, gloomy and complaining. Something called "laughter therapy" has even been developed. One man claims to have cured his cancer by a deliberate program of laughter and humor. "Laughter therapy" promotes the use of books of jokes and humorous stories, living in a kind of party atmosphere and keeping a constant exchange of laughter with family and friends.

I am unsure about the real benefits of such therapy. I would want to stay in harmony with my Christian faith, but I certainly prefer this approach above the gloom-and-doom attitude.

These ideas deal with the psychological question of the power of mind over matter. The beneficial effects of a cheerful spirit have long been known. More recent is the notion that one may "will" specific changes in bodily organs by focusing attention and encouragement on them. For example, I might increase the flow of my pancreatic juices by constantly thinking and imagining the functioning of my pancreas. In other words, I would tell it to "get going." Or I might increase my body's production of red corpuscles by eating a food calculated to help in that process and then imagining the function of that food as it travels to my bone marrow. Again, I do not know how effective such attitudes are, but I find it easy to believe they have potential.

Prayer and Faith

Finally, we must also consider the relationship of prayer and Christian faith to the questions of health and sickness and how we handle them. These are questions for any age, but they arrest us with particular force in our older years as we seek to make closure on our understanding of the meaning and purpose of life. Each new pain and illness seems more fatal and reminds us that our years are growing shorter. Are we as older persons more than in youth supposed to relinquish our grip on life and say, "So be it, even so come Lord Jesus"? There may be a time for that, but we do not come to it soon or easily. That is as it should be.

I observe that for Christians the most common resort in times of illness or affliction is prayer. We believe in it. We have biblical bases for it in both the Old and New Testaments. We have the example and illustration of Jesus' extensive and compassionate ministry to physical need. We have the specific teaching of the New Testament, particularly James 5. Although God is working in an economy in which He clearly leads us to understand that all humankind faces physical death, yet His heart yearns over our suffering, and He has softened the blow as much as possible.

In all the years of my ministry, in all the appeals that people made to me for prayer, by far the largest percentage were prayers for healing. In most cases the request included the clear hope for physical healing, and I never refused them. I am just as prone as anyone else (older people in particular) to regard every new pain or disability as the harbinger of some final and fatal disease. While it may be somewhat contrary to the ideal of calm resignation, whenever I face the crisis of illness in my own life, I take it to the Lord in prayer. However, I always come to one point where I hesitate. When it comes down to asking God to extend my life, I back off and consider. Why should I? What right do I have? Is that what I really want?

Long ago I learned not to bargain with God. In my seminary days, away from home, absent from wife and children and in a hurry to finish my studies, I did as others have done—I over-extended. I became a nervous wreck. I could not sleep. My studies frightened me. I began to fear for my health and well-being. As always, my final response was, "I must take this to the Lord in prayer." Then my rational being took over. "Look," I told myself, "you got yourself into this, what right do you have to ask God to bail you out?" I thought about it for a few days, and an answer came to me. If I only went to the Lord when I had a good case to make, when I could somehow twist His arm, then I would never make it. I would never be worthy of His special favor. I took my problem to the Lord and found grace and healing.

God deals with His children out of loving-kindness. When we are most foolish and undeserving, His loving-kindness shines brightest!

I am satisfied from my understanding of Scripture that God is interested in the physical well being of His children. He teaches us to pray about physical needs as well as spiritual concerns. I believe God makes exceptions to what might appear to be the normal course of natural law—He answers prayer! I suspect God makes many adjustments to our needs even before we ask—adjustments of which we may never be aware.

Currently, I share teaching duties in the men's Bible class of my home congregation. Among ourselves, we call it the

"Old Men's Class." Periodically, we go through a final illness with one of our number. For what do we pray? For physical healing? Yes, but also for much more. We pray for God's reassuring presence with the person and his family. When God's intentions become more clear, we sometimes ask ourselves how long we should continue praying for physical healing. Sometimes we decide to stop praying for healing. But we never stop praying that God will deal gently with our brother and lead him into a glorious home-going. The experience always binds us together, bringing us all closer to each other and closer to our Heavenly Father. It is always appropriate to pray for those who are ill. I remember the words of a song I used to hear:

Lead me gently home, Father,
Lead me gently home;
Lest I fall upon the wayside,
Lead me gently home.[1]

5. Now It's My Turn

Your old men shall dream dreams,
your young men shall see visions.

(Joel 2:28b)

**The old boast that
"the buck stops here"
doesn't mean that the buck
really stops.**

Thomas Jefferson, in a letter to his friend Benjamin Rush, observed, "There is a fullness of time when men should go, and not occupy too long the ground to which others have the right to advance." It is indeed a profound and thought-provoking statement, one to which most of us would subscribe idealistically, but also one from which we might withdraw when the time comes to give up our own toys and let someone else control the game. I find the comment even more remarkable in light of the fact that Jefferson made his observation long before there was any such thing as a retirement age. In fact, Jefferson may have been referring to death rather than retirement.

In the United States we have lived with social security and mandatory retirement just over a generation. During that time, much progress has been made in health care. Longevity and the general activity of older adults both have increased, raising serious questions about the wisdom of using sixty-five as a public mandatory retirement age. In fact, no arbitrary retirement age will ever seem to fit everyone for the simple reason that as individuals we do not "peak" in our maturity and do not decline in our physical and mental capacities at the same rate or the same chronological age.

Individuals now coming to retirement have lived all their working years with the present system of social security and mandatory retirement. It certainly should not surprise them. They have had forty to fifty years to think about and plan for retirement. Still, it does seem to shock many people.

A Time for Retirement

From a purely philosophical understanding of life, we cannot think it strange that as generation succeeds generation, a time arrives for one to lay down responsibilities and honors in order that the next generation may take them up. Trouble ensues when our human nature wants to relinquish power on its own terms—to delay somehow our own individual giving up of the torch.

In the Judeo-Christian tradition, we have been taught to honor and respect old age, to hear the counsel of the elders. This does not mean, however, that older folks should carry either all the responsibilities or all the honors. We Westerners sometimes look critically at the Chinese culture where reverence for age also grants a position of authority to the older person. Carried to its extreme, this has meant that progressive ideas have been forbidden by old men out of touch with reality, and younger men have been denied the power of l̤ea̤d̤e̤r̤ far past their years of maturity.

The opposite is more likely true in our own country where preoccupation with youth—our worship of the youth cult—has made it, if not a crime, then at least a joke to be old. Small wonder that many have been inclined to look at retirement as the end of the line—a jumping into the abyss. Be assured it is not so, and the first line of defense against being surprised, shocked and embittered by the experience is a wholesome understanding of the passages of life. Second, one should realize the possibilities of satisfying and worthwhile activities beyond retirement and prepare ahead of time to grasp those good things.

It is important to fortify our minds with the assurance of the fundamental rightness of moving over to give place to those who are following after. While much may often be desired with regard to the time and manner in which we are asked to give up responsibilities, underneath lies a valid expectation and a fundamental rightness.

When it came time for me to retire from my responsibilities in church administration, I tried to take a fair and sensible look at the situation. One thing struck me forcefully. The persons in line to take the assignments I was releasing were already older than I had been when I began to assume the responsibilities. Why should I be surprised?

One recollection brought mingled feelings. I was serving with the Executive Committee of the Virginia Mennonite Conference. In those days the Executive Committee was responsible for making a number of appointments to church-wide boards and committees, and we often did it rather informally. We might just ask ourselves in free discussion who was available, who had interest in that particular field, who was willing to take the assignment. We seldom even asked those whose names were proposed to "go for a drink" while we decided. On one occasion a seat on the General Council of our national church body needed to be filled. The usual informal discussion finally focused on two names—mine and that of an older brother not too far from retirement. This was my first opportunity for a significant church-wide assignment. At the same time, or maybe it was only later in retrospect, I realized it was his last opportunity. I had no doubts about my own willingness to serve, and with modesty, was confident of my qualification for the task. To be honest, I suppose I was a bit eager. I said nothing to influence the decision one way or another. Presently, the committee gave the assignment to me, and I entered church administration, an area of service that became a large part of my ministry and career. Forty years later I ask myself, "Should I, in deference to the older brother, have urged the assignment on the older man?"

It Isn't Easy

I do not mean to say that retirement is, or should be, easy and without trauma. Something about being busy, being involved in significant work, feeling that we are making worthwhile contributions to the well-being of our family, church and community satisfies and gives a sense of fulfillment and purpose in living. To be separated from this, perhaps suddenly as it seems at retirement, is understandably traumatic. Elise Maclay's poem "I Miss Being Needed" says it well.

I miss being needed.
Once the whole family depended on me.
I was the breadwinner.
Only I didn't win the bread, I worked hard and earned it.
When I picked up my paycheck, I was proud.
I didn't mind that it went for the family.

I was proud to buy shoes, a Flexible Flyer sled, a
    college education.
I was needed at work.
In the community.
At home.
To build and haul.
To serve on committees.
To decide things.
To help people out.
Sometimes I'd get exasperated and say, Does the
    whole world have to lean on me?
Now I wish somebody would.
The trouble is, now that I'm old, people have no idea
    what I'm good for.
Well, neither do I.
But I can find out.
Maybe to be needed, a man doesn't always have to be
    doing something.
He can just be there.
Like a star.
A fixed point.
For others to take their bearings from.[1]

Because my own experience of retirement has been positive, I may not be best qualified to give consolation and
direction to those who have experienced retirement as a severe
trauma. I grew up on a farm and later spent a few years as a
bench mechanic in the sheet metal trade, doing some traveling
as an installer of heating and ventilating equipment. For most
of my adult life, however, I worked as a pastor, college
professor and, finally, church administrator in the office of
bishop. My last three professions were not strictly successive
but somewhat overlapping. I was fortunate to have at least

moderate opportunities for travel as well. All this gave me a rich background from which to draw for reflection and conversation in my retirement years.

Retirement at Eastern Mennonite College and Seminary came at sixty-five. No sweat. I was glad to be free of the schedule of classes and student appointments which I carried as registrar. Not that I didn't miss the routine and the contacts, but I was given a new freedom for work in the church which I felt had occasionally been neglected in favor of my academic responsibilities.

For whatever reasons, the people who formulated the retirement policies of Virginia Mennonite Conference set the retirement age for bishops at seventy. In the practical outworking of assignments in the district where I served as bishop, I was not free of responsibilities until I was seventy-two. Shortly thereafter I was asked to serve with our Conference Older Adults Ministries Committee. Hence, I have a sort of post-retirement career. In addition and by request, I also stayed on several other committees for a time. I suspect the real reason for my continuing committee assignments resulted from my willingness to be a sucker for secretarial duties. Through the years, it seemed whenever I showed up at a committee or board meeting, everyone breathed a sigh of relief and by voice or vote said, "Linden will take the minutes."

My wife, Esther, has had similar retirement experiences. When she retired from being Librarian at Eastern Mennonite High School, she found herself besieged with all sorts of voluntary service projects for which she had no time before. She did a turn with the auxiliary of the Virginia Mennonite Retirement Community, read and evaluated books for the Choice Books program, worked in a Gift and Thrift store and did a stint with the Women's Missionary and Service Commission as Secretary of Literature, which included a task at which we worked together—gathering, sorting and packing Sunday school literature to be shipped to churches in Jamaica.

Together we identified with several para-church organizations which, being entirely voluntary, asked no questions about age. On top of everything, I had the inclination to do a bit of writing, some by request and some on my own. If all this sounds a bit ambitious, remember we weren't doing all these things simultaneously. But we have kept busy. There has never been a time in the thirteen years since I "began" to retire when I woke up in the morning to ask myself what I would do today. Now, when friends ask Esther and me what we do in our retirement, we are apt to ask, "What retirement?" My friend, John Mumaw, has a word of warning, however, about those who retire and brag about being busier than they were before. "What they don't realize," says John, "is that it just takes them longer to do things than it ever did before."

I sometimes chuckle about a little joke I played on myself. Shortly before retirement, I bought myself a small estate-type tractor equipped with mower, bottom plow, tiller, snow blade and cart. The argument that once I retired I would have a lot of time on my hands satisfied my wife and persuaded my own conscience to spend the money. I could make a profitable sideline of plowing and tilling gardens and cleaning snow from driveways. An older man in our neighborhood had done just that, and I would be set to take his place.

Well, I made good use of the mower, but mostly in my own sizeable yard. I occasionally cleaned a few of my neighbors' driveways, but not for pay. I plowed my own garden, but those I plowed for pay could be counted on the fingers of one hand. I finally sold the tiller since I had no time to use it. I still think it was a good idea—for someone whose retirement needs and activities are a bit different than my own.

Lest I paint an unrealistically rosy picture of retirement, let me summarize a bit. I admit I was fortunate, more fortunate than many who find themselves with empty hands after retirement. Almost, but not entirely, without direction or effort on my part, I was given opportunities in line with my interests. Even so, leaving a position which had given me identity, status and a sense of fulfillment was not totally without trauma. I, too, experienced a sense of loss and the necessity of sometimes painful adjustment.

Upon retirement, many of us are shocked to find ourselves out of touch with our familiar world. At Eastern Mennonite College and Seminary, my responsibilities in administration kept me in touch with what was going on around campus. Not that I had a part in all decisions, but I was in the know. Once retired, I no longer had access to the day-by-day problems, decisions and plans. Students that I had known were soon gone from campus. In a surprisingly short time, I found myself rather painlessly detached from campus life. I attended faculty social functions for a while but gradually dropped most of them.

It was a bit different when I retired from my duties as bishop. In giving up that office, I also gave up my seat on the Virginia Conference Council on Faith and Life. The Council reviewed practically all activities of the Conference, made many decisions on policy and was involved in securing and assigning personnel. Once off the Council, I soon felt out of touch with the throb of life, with elements that had been my responsibility, challenge and concern for many years. For the first time, I really felt I had retired.

On one occasion I shared my feelings with friend Barbara Reber who at that point was working with the Inter-Mennonite Council on Aging. Barbara listened sympathetically and then said with all seriousness, "You are certainly entitled to a time of grieving over that loss." Her words shocked me a bit. I had not thought of what was happening to me as grieving. Then I remembered that grieving was a very prominent word in the literature on aging. We not only grieve over death and the loss of loved ones. We grieve over the loss of many other things— possessions, positions, powers, physical functions and a host of others. In the prime of life, we may not quite understand this, and in age we may be ashamed to admit it. Grieving, however, should not be thought of as the measure of our loss. It is rather a process of healing, an aid to the necessary adjustments, a finding and gearing up for new and worthwhile things ahead.

Surrendering Control

Surrendering the sense of responsibility, the concern for the ongoing success of whatever was the central focus of our lives looms as a second hurdle for many retirees. This is particularly true for those who have been immersed in church vocations or who have built successful family businesses. It is true also for those who have been in education, a professional group or any corporate venture. I will refrain from telling any specific stories about family problems of keeping Grandpa, who founded the business, from still making decisions and telling the help what to do when the responsibilities have long been officially assigned to a son or daughter. It isn't easy for either generation, and there are no magical solutions. What we need is the wisdom to recognize not only the inevitability of the passing of generations, but also its fundamental rightness. Hopefully, we will have the wisdom to take retirement as a release from responsibility, a time for new ventures, a time for reflection and assessment of the meaning of life.

I remember the story of the seventy-year-old son and the ninety-year-old mother who came to hot disagreement over how to season the family's kettle of apple butter simmering over the open fire. When the son finally prevailed over the mother's protests, she closed with a parting shot, "When you get a little older, you will know better."

I thought I had worked through the problems of retirement carefully. I had plans for the future. I recognized the rightness of it. I had tried to carry my assignments faithfully. I was ready to turn responsibility over to younger men. Guess what? As I watched younger men take over the responsibilities I had had, I discovered one day that I had settled on two of them for a bit of resentment. I didn't think it was in me, but I could not deny that the little green-eyed monster sat on my shoulder. It was totally irrational, but I suppose perfectly human. The two in question were my friends. They had been respectful of my seniority and personally supportive. I took immediate steps to put that bit of jealousy out of my heart.

Relinquishing responsibility, even when one is prepared and has acknowledged its rightness, does not necessarily take away the continuing personal concern for a cause that has been next to the heart for years. My predecessor in the bishop office was J. Ward Shank. He was my mentor, and we worked together agreeably for a number of years. When it came time for him to retire, he did it graciously and with dignity. While he never let the shadow of his past authority fall on my path, I knew Ward continued to carry a heavy concern for the work of the church in our district. One day he came to me in a good mood. It seemed his countenance was lifted. In the course of conversation he said, "The Lord has shown me that He no longer holds me responsible for everything that happens in the church." It was for him a freeing experience and a conversation which I later remembered.

The buck stops here. How long has that little reminder stood on your desk? It is not only for bishops, college presidents and corporate executives. Every one of us in the course of our working lives has been assigned some area of responsibility. We are expected to have the answers in certain situations. In retirement we can take the sign off our desk. Someone else must now intercept the buck.

To most people this experience comes as a sort of mixed bag. To some the loss of authority, loss of the sense of usefulness, loss of a familiar routine and even loss of identity seems overwhelming. They never get beyond it but settle into a swamp of resentment and bitterness. To others, who have cultivated a better understanding of the place of retirement in a whole life experience and who have planned for a continuing life of significant activity, this laying down of responsibility can be one of the most freeing and exhilarating experiences of life. Neither our bodies, minds or emotions are constructed for perpetual wear. One can bear the "burden and heat of the day" for only so long. To hand over our responsibilities to "those who are coming after" with grace and confidence signals maturity, the sign of a job well done.

It will be frustrating to watch people "make mistakes" and "do things wrong" in a cause to which we have given the best of our life. (It helps to imagine how the person felt who watched one's own fledgling efforts to bring the ship into a steady course.) I hope I never cease to care and to be deeply concerned about things which happen in the college and the church where I gave the earnest efforts of my working years. While I sometimes feel there is reason to be concerned, I also confess a real sense of release and a deep sense of peace that I am no longer held responsible for decisions and their out-come.

Using the Wisdom of Age
Perhaps I tread on dangerous ground and my remarks about no longer being responsible may provoke violent reaction in

some minds. Yes, there is a time for us older ones to speak. There is a legacy of wisdom and experience which wise children will not want to shove aside. Again from Job, "Wisdom is with aged men, and with length of days understanding" (Job 12:12). If I had been the translator, I might have slipped "sometimes" into the margin. Nevertheless, we have the divine word, indicating the normal expectation. Any people are the poorer who do not take advantage of the store of wisdom and experience in their midst.

For better or worse, right or wrong, our culture has set a time for authority and responsibility to be transferred. Those who try to hold onto the reins which by formal decree and common expectation have been passed on to others only make themselves unhappy. J. Ward Shank was right when he perceived the Lord no longer held him responsible.

I indicated earlier that my years of retirement have been filled with rewarding activity. I am busy. I have deadlines to meet. However, I am much less bound to the calendar and the clock. The committee and personal appointments are much more of my choosing. Deadlines for completion of work are more flexible. The pace of life is more leisurely, and I have time for reflection. Even Bible reading and study have taken on new dimensions. I once did Bible studies urgently to fulfill my obligation to the students coming through my classes— sometimes to keep ahead of them. I studied the Bible in preparation for sermons I did weekly. Now I have time to read the Bible meditatively for my own pleasure and spiritual edification. It has added a whole new dimension to my life.

Esther and I usually get up at the same time we have been getting up for years, but if for any reason we want to, we can sleep in a while. We watch for music events coming to our area and take time to go. We have a fascination for the West Virginia hills, having lived there for ten years. If we feel like taking a day off just to wander aimlessly (by car) over those hils, either alone or with another couple, we can do it. And still we tell ourselves we are not getting everything done we would like. Particularly, we would do more visitation of shut-ins, the bereaved or just old friends. Life definitely moves at a different pace.

The retiree must be prepared to downscale his or her expectations. The retiring teacher may find opportunity to tutor slow learners or maybe newly-arrived refugees. The accountant may volunteer to manage the finances of someone newly widowed or an otherwise needy person. The successful contractor may offer to supervise the repair or rebuilding of houses damaged or destroyed by some natural disaster. Such opportunities provide occupation in one's familiar field of interest and expertise. They may not carry the same level of authority or public notice, but neither do they require the same outlay of energy in the world's competitive market. Many are ideally fitted to declining physical and emotional stamina. This is the leisure of retirement. Amazingly, the satisfaction and rewards for continued activity and worthwhile service are often no less than the former sense of achievement in one's chosen vocation.

When I retired from my responsibilities at the conference and national church level, my wife and I went back to what had been my home congregation since childhood. Almost at once we were plunged into activities at the congregational level much like the ones I had carried on the conference level. While this has run its course in the extended years of retirement, we both continue to teach Sunday school classes of our own peers. The ongoing challenge of theological scholarship and the close-knit fellowship of the class I teach has been one of the most truly satisfying experiences of all my years.

Lately, at the encouragement of others, Esther and I agreed

to shepherd a little church in the West Virginia hills. It is a very small group, not financially able to hire a regular pastor. We only go once or twice a month to share with the people, but it affords rich friendships and keeps alive and fulfills my life-long love of the pastorate.

Retirement is not the end of the line. Rather it may be a sort of crest in the long grade, a place to shift gears for easing gently into the home station.

6. Taking the Plunge

For the children ought not to lay up for the parents but the parents for the children.

(II Corinthians 12:14b)

"A penny saved is a penny earned." —Ben Franklin

When I was a boy, my brother and I, sometimes with friends, would occasionally "skinny-dip" in Linville Creek which ran through our father's farm. We stood on the bank of the cold spring-fed stream, making ready for the dive. We much preferred taking a deep breath and plunging in because wading in meant cold water crept up our bodies inch by inch. The thought of the cold water on bare skin often meant we exhaled that first breath and maybe a couple more before actually taking the plunge. Once in the water, the capillaries of the skin quickly adjusted. We were set for a nice leisurely swim.

Retirement is much like that plunge into the "ole swimming hole," sometimes in a very positive way and sometimes in a negative way. How one responds to the plunge depends largely on the degree of understanding and preparation.

Anticipation of Retirement

Many persons have anticipated retirement as the day of release from the daily grind of work, responsibility and confinement. They will be free to do as they choose. Leisure will be endless. Enjoyment will be assured and spontaneous.

Others prefer not to retire. They enjoy the security and satisfaction of work. They hold places of prestige and authority which they do not want to give up. They do not believe their physical powers are, or soon will be, diminishing. They must, in the words of one writer, be dragged "kicking and screaming" into retirement. The waters of their spring-fed stream never seem to warm.

Smooth retirement requires acceptance and planning. The starry-eyed view of retirement as the day of release guarantees disappointment. The waters one thought to be so inviting may turn out to be chilly. Leisure may become a tyrant. One can only go fishing or golfing so many days a week until it becomes stale. Moreover, the new and unaccustomed proximity of husband and wife may create hassles. Stubborn refusal to acknowledge retirement as fundamentally right is equally foolish and can only lead to fruitless brooding.

Financial Realities

Lack of money to live the life anticipated presents one of the most common sources of frustration and disappointment in retirement. Building a hedge against that particular pitfall demands thought and planning ahead of time—far ahead. I will not attempt in this book to give counsel on money management and investments. Many such books have been written by persons far more qualified in economics than myself. Much good advice is available, both through written materials and through qualified personal financial counselors. My message is simple. Do something about it. Reckon with your probable financial needs before the retirement party— long before.

We live in a consumer-oriented society. People are encouraged to live beyond their means. Our credit card mentality makes that easy. An amazing number of people encourage me to enhance my image by subscribing to their particular charge card. Thanks, but no thanks. I have only two cards other than my telephone credit card. I want no more.

What we desperately need today are more simple lifestyles and more disciplined family economic structures, including definite savings accounts of one type or another. Surprisingly, a regular savings account at compound interest grows into a substantial auxiliary income by retirement time. I remember the girl who bragged to her friends about an uncle who had lots of money. "How did your uncle make his money?" one of the friends asked. "Oh, oh, well," she stammered, "he kept it."

One of the fallacies which has tripped up far too many is the myth that Social Security and Medicare provide financial security for old age. From its beginning, Social Security was not intended to furnish a secure living, only supplemental income. So prevalent is the notion that Medicare covers all medical and hospital bills and even includes long-term nursing home care, that I would advise everyone to make sure they have adequate and up-to-date information on Medicare and Medicaid. Medicare does not cover all medical and hospital costs and allows almost nothing for nursing home care. Some kind of supplemental insurance is a necessity.

I consider long-term care insurance an "iffy" issue. It is currently very expensive for the individual and not too attractive to insurance carriers. Some initial attempts proved unsatisfactory, both to the insured and the insurers. However, its need is rather pressing, and newer plans are being worked on diligently. Who needs it and for whom is it a good investment?

One financial counselor outlined it for me. If one is sufficiently wealthy, having enough income to pay for a stay in a nursing home without depleting the estate, it is best to forego the insurance and take the chance of not spending a long time in a nursing home.

If financial assets are relatively modest so that even the insurance premium depletes the estate, once again one should forget it and, if worse comes to worst, simply fall back on Medicaid.

However, should one be in the medium bracket of financial well-being and able to afford the annual premium out of earned income without depleting the estate, perhaps long-term care insurance is a good investment.

With the exception of those who are truly rich, most people have three primary sources of retirement income—Social Security (including Medicare), pensions and investment income (including property).

As noted earlier, Social Security was not intended to support retirees in financial independence. However, growing pressures on the "welfare state" and strong lobbies advocating concerns of the elderly in Congress have made Social Security a very substantial and dependable base of operation for the American elderly. Particularly when both husband and wife have worked in the public market and have independent accounts, Social Security supplies a comfortable financial base. I recommend knowing the amount of your entitlement and checking to be sure your account is in proper order when you sit down to calculate retirement income.

Pension plans have been more tricky. Those who have worked for government agencies at either national, state or municipal levels have become heirs of generous pension plans to the point it threatens to become a scandal and a financial threat to the economy. Municipal workers in some areas boast that their take-home pay after retirement is better than during their working years.

While business and industry have also been generous with retirement benefits, the situation is more tenuous than with government workers. Government agencies guarantee their pension plans with tax money. In the private sector pension plans depend on the financial health of the economy. In hard times they may become a threat to the financial stability of a private business. In cases of bankruptcy, takeovers or mergers, pension plans are sometimes lost or unfairly altered. Unscrupulous businesses have changed their rules about continuity or length of employment as it affected the individual worker's pension claims. In recent years many workers have been severely disappointed and their hopes and plans dashed when they found their pension expectations had been unknowingly and unfairly changed. Again, it seems important to check this frequently and to verify it before you retire.

Savers and Spenders

The third source of retirement income depends largely on your private initiative and discipline through the years. True, some people, through no fault of their own, are unable to lay up large savings during their working years. Family misfortunes, sickness with its attendant medical bills, fires or other natural disasters and even lack of employment may forbid the normal growth of family savings.

More often the lack of foresight and discipline has prevented the development of a family nest egg. According to financial analysts, Americans, though noted for thriftiness and "making do," have not generally been adequate "savers." Too often when available cash increased, so did the living standard. Most North Americans follow a lifestyle which always demands "just a little more" and which the credit card makes easy.

For those who have had the foresight to save, investment in property has been a favorite. In a rising economy, appreciation increases personal assets and income at a relatively rapid rate. Even in a static economy, real estate is a solid hedge against loss. In the matter of retirement income, real property which provides rental income may be a welcome supplement or a major base which determines the retirement lifestyle, the fulfillment of dreams. Others may elect to invest in stocks or bonds. For example, mutual funds and growth stocks have been sound investments for a long period and continue to be recommended.

In my opinion certificates of deposits or regular savings accounts still represent the most secure investment, though not always the most profitable since interest rates may fluctuate. You can allow the account to accumulate simply by compounding the interest (adding it to the account). At retirement you may wish to have the account converted into one which enhances your income by paying monthly interest. Of course, if you prefer, you may receive the interest on a monthly or quarterly basis from the beginning. The secret to any savings plan is to begin early and to follow it diligently. Waiting until retirement practically assures the impossibility of building a really helpful interest income.

To assess your financial resources carefully, followed by building or trimming your expectations accordingly, is an important pre-retirement exercise. Better a facing the facts up front than a devastating letdown later.

Where Will You Live?
Another major consideration for the near-retiree is housing. For the majority of persons, retirement will not signal an

immediate change of residence. Most homeowners will elect to stay put at least for the immediate future. Doing some repairs or alterations and a new interest in lawn or garden may well be at least a part of the retirement therapy. However, it may be good to look ahead. Are there financial possibilities in the large house once needed to accommodate a growing family? How about an apartment? Will the lawn and garden, now a hobby, become a burden; the house too much care for declining energies? What are the predictions in your neighborhood regarding property values over the next few years?

Those persons who eagerly awaited retirement time to head for the warm and sunny climate of Florida or Arizona may want to reconsider. Have you actually spent enough time there to be sure you will like it? Will you be happy? Would it be wise to try it a year before disposing of your property in your home state?

A few people have believed the right investment for retirement might be a mobile home. Supposedly, it affords the once-in-a-lifetime opportunity to visit in leisurely fashion all those scenic or historically interesting places one always wanted to visit. Furthermore, with a motor home one can flow with the seasons and the birds, taking advantage of the ideal weather locations all year long. The consensus of recent opinion suggests that even this idyllic life gets old. Most people eventually want a settled community where they can make friends, develop a support group, establish credit and find a medical home base. If you are tempted with this dream, calculate your finances carefully and do not get caught in a situation from which you cannot back out.

Most people retiring around age sixty-five will have a few more years to consolidate their resources and contemplate some change of housing. Retirement centers in many communities offer various options—cottages, owned apartments, rented apartments, dormitory-type adult homes and, finally, nursing homes. In many cases one can buy into a package which supplies these accommodations successively as needed. The packages usually include gradual relief from the responsibilities of lawn care, upkeep of buildings and paying taxes and monthly bills—light, heat, maybe even telephone. Further, they always offer security. With all the attractions of retirement home care, current wisdom of those in the elder care field still recommends that independent living be maintained as long as possible, either in the old family home or in an apartment. The message to the new retiree seems to be, "Do look ahead, but take your time and consider carefully."

Prepare for Some Surprises

Likely the most important, or at least most immediate, question for the new retiree will be, "How do I fill my time?"

I have been doing everything possible to build up retirement as a potentially new and exciting chapter in life.

However, prepare yourself for a few jolts and necessary adjustments. Most of us, even though we may at times badmouth the daily grind, do become comfortable with a regular routine and will probably miss it. At work we have friends with whom we feel at ease, share responsibility and whom we will miss as we move out of the circle.

Do not be surprised if you experience some letdown, even feel depressed. As my friend Barbara once told me, "You are entitled to a period of grieving." If perchance you approached retirement with a measure of euphoria as the day of release, do not give up when you hit the doldrums. With acceptance and a forward look, your new situation will become all that you expected. Fighting the system is futile. You cannot change society. The fifteen, twenty or more years beyond sixty-five that many, many retirees will enjoy is time enough for some genuine and significant achievements and a lot of good living.

Don't expect people to keep on remembering all your notable exploits once they have been duly recited at your retirement party. It will be done again at your funeral, so don't be in a hurry! It is up to you to keep on doing things which give you a sense of satisfaction and usefulness, a new status and identity. I am not saying that you should give up your memories nor throw away all your citations and keepsakes. They can be rehearsed and even displayed among family and friends. But do be aware that the world moves on; others take your place and have their time for achievement and authority.

Not long ago Esther and I went to a dedication service in a church in an adjoining community to celebrate the completion of additional facilities for an expanding program. Thirty years before, I had preached the dedication sermon for the original building and had served as non-resident overseer for most of the next twenty-five years. I anticipated that as "the old bishop" I would be asked for a "few words of greeting" and perhaps a little time to reminisce. I was prepared to share with them a few inside stories which were not public knowledge at the time of their happening.

Well, we were warmly greeted by old friends, enjoyed the program and had a thoroughly good time. But there was no place on the well-ordered program for my reminiscences. I must acknowledge a bit of disappointment. Then I remembered I was writing a book about climbing down the ladder. "This is it," I told myself. "This is what you have been talking about."

As I analyzed the situation, I realized I had been pretty well out of sight for the past six or seven years. New persons had come into places of leadership. New persons had engineered the achievements that were being celebrated, and they deserved the recognition they were given. Esther and I are still basking in the warmth of the hugs, smiles and words of appreciation from old friends who had shared with us the struggles and triumphs of days past.

Keeping in Touch

One serious problem many new retirees face is a sense that they are losing touch with what had been important in life. Whether leaving a business establishment, separating from a professional group or dropping out of public service, one soon feels separated from the former life. For some it is a very devastating feeling. My own lifework was primarily with the church. More than a means of livelihood, it was a cause to which I had utterly dedicated myself—the upbuilding of the Kingdom of God. As long as I live, I will be interested in it, will still want to do more. I do not want to be out of touch.

Having said this about my own situation, I recognize that each of us may feel the same way about our own particular life's work. We have every right to be interested in and concerned about it to the end of our days.

Regarding suggestions for keeping in touch, I have not been able to come up with too many alternatives. One of the disciplines of retirement is simply that of acceptance, to trust the torch of responsibility to other hands without resentment and without undue fear. There are other things to which we may now give our attention.

For almost every trade, profession and hobby, there are journals and other literature. These afford an excellent way of keeping abreast of change and progress in any area of interest. Many of us will want to read such literature even though we are no longer directly involved in or dependent on a given enterprise for our livelihood. It remains a matter of satisfaction to be able to converse knowledgeably, to keep up with new advances in an area of lifelong interest.

Another source is to cultivate friends, particularly younger ones, who are still in the field. They can keep you abreast of developments and may value the help you can give them out of your years of knowledge and experience. For example, I have a good friend named Sam Weaver. Years ago I was instrumental in bringing Sam into the ministry and involvement in church work. We have been good friends and colleagues for a long time. Currently, Sam is Executive Secretary of our church conference. When I can find a spot on his busy schedule, I take Sam out to breakfast. He fills me in on current activities and issues. Barring items under advisement and pending official action, he is free to share with me. Not infrequently, he suggests the things that need my prayers. He often makes my day by asking my advice on thorny current issues. The cost of breakfast is a small price to pay for the wholeness of being kept on the cutting edge.

7. The Time Factor

To everything there is a season,
a time for every purpose under the heaven.

(Ecclesiastes 3:1)

People in prison
are probably the only ones
who wish they had
less "time."

I scarcely know who is most to be pitied—the man who can't get out of bed in the morning or the man who has no reason to get out of bed. In my opinion, men are much more likely to be unmotivated in this way than women. Women, as long as they have a house to live in—even a tiny apartment—and meals to make—even for themselves—will feel some reason for getting out of bed in the morning. A man who at retirement has just lost his identity, his sense of worth and a base of operation is much more likely to question the wisdom of getting up in the morning. The man who has nothing more to look forward to than the morning paper, the television, a soft drink (or a can of beer) and a bag of potato chips, who has no reason to shave because he is "not going to see anybody," is indeed to be pitied.

It is easy to say that such a situation is the result of not planning ahead, of not thinking how the hours, days and years of retirement are going to be filled. Many are tempted to feel that deliverance from the tyranny of the time clock will be paradise and fishing every day will be heaven itself. Usually, it does not turn out that way. It is just as important to think ahead about how to occupy one's time as it is to plan ahead about where and on what finances one will live.

Buying Time with Retirement Alternatives

I return to the point of looking retirement squarely in the eye before the day arrives. In the past few years, new laws have somewhat relieved the strict retirement- at-sixty-five requirement. You may be in the position to negotiate for additional work time if that is really what you want. If your finances will be tight, that might even be a wise move since the extra time will increase the amount of Social Security once you do retire.

In other cases it may be possible to negotiate for part-time work, thus affording relief from a full load of responsibility while providing continued contact with a familiar life-pattern, some financial remuneration and some leisure time. Again, it may be possible to remain with one's business or professional connection as a consultant, affording all the above benefits plus a new, respected status.

Earlier I spoke of my own good fortune in being able to retire in stages. Having carried responsibility in several different areas, I did not give up everything at once. At each stage, I surrendered certain responsibilities while also finding relief from certain stresses. At the same time I retained some significant work in which I was interested. I call that coming down the ladder rung by rung rather than jumping off. Not everyone can hope to be so fortunate.

Of course, taking lesser assignments can be hard on one's pride and depends largely on personal acceptance and adjustment. I remember an older man whom I consider one of my mentors who often said of certain assignments and opportunities, "That job is just as big as you are willing to make it." In fairness, I do also realize not everyone will have the opportunity to taper off responsibilities the way I did, but it may be worth a try.

Second Careers

Much has been written and said lately about second and third careers. Persons who retire at sixty-five or younger may easily have half as much time left for a second career as they spent in the first. While some may have changed careers several times during the course of a working life, "second career" for my purposes means something one takes up following retirement. Compared to "hobby," "second career" sounds like a serious venture—something requiring a major portion of time and which serves as a source of continuing income.

Many persons cherish for years the dream of someday being "in business for themselves," and retirement supplies the opportune moment for such a venture. The choices are as broad as the scope of money-making enterprises. However, it is important to explore well the cost of launching such a venture, its probability of success in the particular community and how much determination it will take to see such a project through.

Recently the fields of insurance and real estate have attracted a number of my friends into second careers. The trick is to qualify before retirement as a salesman in one of these fields. There is always the opportunity to become an independent operator—to own one's own business.

In a less ambitious vein, one might start his or her own bookkeeping, accounting or tax service business. Someone with a more mechanical inclination might try turning out wooden toys or lawn ornaments from a home workshop, simply allowing demand, financial involvement and personal inclination to determine if it becomes a business or remains a hobby. Every community needs one or more handyman operators—nothing heavy—just a fixer of light switches, locks, leaky faucets and cranky window blinds. A bit more ambitious would be a repair shop for small electrical appliances or small motors.

Hobbies

Hobbies enrich all ages and all stages of life. In fact, it is important to develop hobbies early in life. Great stress-relievers, they serve to soothe the tedium of daily routine and take the mind off the unpleasant disappointments or irritations of the workplace. Hobbies can be very costly, moderately costly, modestly profitable or even occasionally very profitable. Most of us will pay modestly for our hobbies. We do not expect the payoff to be financial, rather we derive from them enjoyment and pleasure. Hobbies add wholeness to life.

For a hobby to be a part of the therapy of retirement, it must be in place beforehand. To tell oneself the morning after the retirement party "Now I must go out and find myself a hobby" is too late. Indeed, it will add to the frustration rather than soothe it.

However, during retirement hobbies often come into their full glory. First of all, they fill the time which may suddenly become such a frightening void. A hobby may be the "security blanket" which preserves one's sense of worth, satisfies the need for creativity and puts one in touch with other people. At this time, also, many people decide whether a hobby remains just that—a source of personal enjoyment and satisfaction— or whether by chance it offers an open door to a second career and a source of financial security.

To begin enumerating hobby ideas is much like "carrying coals to Newcastle." The list is endless. Few of us will become collectors of fine art or restorers of old mansions with their period furniture and living accommodations. But in our spare time, we may be privileged to enjoy the fruits of these hobby-ists, many of whom are often generous public benefactors.

Bluebloods among the collectors are the gatherers of coins and stamps. In the hands of the experienced, these can some-times turn into income sources. From here out, collecting becomes as varied as each person's own interests—anything from baseball cards, comic books or matchbooks to signed pottery, depression glass or first edition books. There are serious collectors of antiques—furniture, glassware or art. Many persons will just want a few family heirlooms. In any case, collecting can be fun. It takes time and often offers interesting social contacts. Personally, I never became a seri-ous collector, though I did have a passing interest in the glass and porcelain insulators which once adorned telephone and electric poles all over the countryside. Later I took a fancy to milk bottles signed in raised glass with the name of the dairy farmer who bottled the milk. These likewise seem to be a thing of the past.

Many hobbies which require physical exertion are also popular among both men and women. Golf, tennis, hunting, fishing, hiking, photography and gardening often head the list. Gardening offers specialties—raising a particular flower such as roses, tulips or whatever is popular. Other gardening specialties include raising herbs or seeds of exotic or "old time" vegetable varieties.

For years when I answered resumes or questionnaires calling for a list of hobbies, I filled in with gardening, fishing and photography. It has been interesting to watch some changes in myself as I grow older. While we were raising a family of hungry children, the garden was a matter of self-preservation—preservation of the pocketbook, that is. When we finally found ourselves alone, Esther and I continued to plant a big garden as a matter of course. We gave the produce away—to the children and the neighbors. We still canned and froze enough in one year to last us for three. Lately I have been saying, "Now this year I'm going to cut down on the garden," and my wife agrees. But when planting time comes, I get carried away, and the garden is as big as ever. I'm beginning to wonder if my garden is a hobby or a compulsion. At any rate, it remains the best way I know to unwind after a tension-building day.

Photography and fishing I take more in stride. My purposes for pursuing photography have changed somewhat from a few years ago. Once a teaching aide, pure personal pleasure now drives it. As for fishing, my knees won't take wading rocky mountain streams for trout as they once did, and Esther wants only so many fish in the freezer. Nonetheless, I still enjoy it and usually tell my friends I am "way behind with my fishing."

A few years ago, even before retirement, Esther and I began to add "travel" to our list of hobbies. Travel can certainly be a great source of pleasure and enrichment. It does require money and a reasonable degree of stamina. We enjoy driving by car and have, in fact, been in all the forty-eight contiguous states. But with increasing years, eyesight dims and our reaction time slows down. I don't mind admitting that the driving I once thoroughly enjoyed has become a bit scary in strange cities and on some interstate highways. Now I say, "Let someone else do the driving." Today, nearly every community offers bus tours lasting from a day to a month and covering every kind of entertainment and all possible points of interest. These bus tours, carefully selected, can be very rewarding.

Almost to my surprise, we have finally added "reading" to our list of hobbies. I ask myself how that could be when almost all my life I made my living, clothed my family and rendered my contribution to the well-being of those around me by reading, studying and pushing pencils. I always did a certain amount of reading for pleasure. Now I find my approach quite different. The "for pleasure" part has increased. I am more relaxed. My purposes are quite different. In life there are, and ought to be, changes which can make it progressively fulfilling.

The World of Voluntary Service

Hats off to volunteerism! A host of good things happen in the world because people volunteer. Many people work tirelessly, doing good to others without expecting pay, sometimes even providing their own living expenses. They volunteer out of the goodness of their hearts and out of their own need to feel useful.

Volunteerism knows no age limits, but in my mind, it is the particular province of the elderly and provides one of the best antidotes I know for retirement blues and the sense of uselessness which plagues so many retirees. I think everyone sometime in life ought to do some voluntary service. What better way to make our older years significant? It is a loving way to say "thank you" to people for the kindnesses we have received in our lifetime, to pay tribute to the community which has given us space in which to live and work and to build up a church where we have found a spiritual home and nurture.

Many women in the business or professional world find upon retirement, for the first time in their lives, they are free to really give time and energy to the Women's Auxiliary program of some institution or join the Women's Missionary and Service Commission of their church. Those whose motherly instincts prompt them to leave a legacy of a hand-stitched quilt (or something comparable) to each of the children and grandchildren will now find time to complete the loving dream.

As I muse over the possibilities of voluntary service (VS) for seniors, I am amazed how few are exclusively male or female. My friend Monroe, who found himself restricted from former activity, has stitched a well-deserved reputation in needlework. Since fewer eyebrows are raised by the fact that men do things traditionally done by women and women do things done by men, husband and wife today can enjoy activities together. In my own circle of friends, I know a lot of instances when just that is happening.

Hospitals have a variety of volunteer opportunities for both men and women. Every community needs teachers' aides and tutors for children with educational disabilities, for children from delinquent home situations or for refugees learning English. For those whose experience has been with money, volunteers are needed to do bookkeeping, file taxes and give financial counsel to the widowed or disabled elderly. Many communities have a representative payee program in which the local court, or a social agency, appoints a volunteer to handle the finances of those who, for whatever reason, are unable to manage their own financial affairs. Gift and Thrift stores, specializing either in used furniture, appliances and clothing at prices the needy can afford or in crafts from third world countries as an overseas relief project, always need volunteers. Skills for selling, for repairing furniture and appliances, for sorting, mending and pricing clothing are all useful.

Another open door of a bit more strenuous kind for volunteers provides disaster relief and housing for the poverty stricken. Here again the opportunities are wide open for both men and women. In the case of fire and flood, lots of clean-up and repair must take place before rebuilding can begin. Sorting and distribution of food and clothing along with the preparation and serving of food in temporary shelters usually demands many volunteer hours. In construction and repair of houses, it is not only skilled carpenters who are needed but painters and interior decorators as well. More and more women are becoming involved in disaster relief, filling traditional roles as cooks, painters and cleaners, but also occasionally working alongside men as carpenters and construction workers.

While disaster relief may first invoke the vision of strong men and machines, recent experience proves it is a fruitful field for retirees because of their availability and their broad range of skills and experience. Retirees have a great deal to offer almost any relief project. Since strength and speed are not usually the main considerations, more and more projects consider the qualifications and experience of seniors. These assignments may range in time from one day to three months and may be done with or without leaving home.

Anyone with a car will find plenty of good deeds available. People who no longer own cars still need transportation to the doctor, lawyer, dentist or hospital. They need to shop, and they may want to visit friends. Other volunteer opportunities include regularly scheduled visits to shut-ins. An arrangement with a nursing home or a church program takes into consideration how much time you have and makes such a service a well-regulated routine. And most communities now have a program of providing meals to the homebound. "Meals on

Wheels," or whatever it may be called, may help satisfy the need to be serving.

A Time to Relax

Does it take twenty-four hours of frantic activity to keep North Americans happy, even in old age? It seems so sometimes. I, for one, thought retirement was a time when we could slow down a bit, relax from the burden of carrying the world on our shoulders and do some of the things we always wanted, but never had time, to do. I have believed, and still do, that in retirement there ought to be time for relaxation and reflection, time to put things in perspective, time to savor life's good experiences and mollify its disappointments. There ought to be space in life to just sit and think—or, if one prefers, to just sit.

I am well aware of the old adage with which the "never done" saints justify themselves, "It is better to wear out than to rust out." That, I submit, is more pious than practical. Jesus Himself invited the disciples to "come apart and rest awhile." Rest has its place. But don't misunderstand my argument. I also know what the Bible has to say about the lazy person—the sluggard—and I believe every bit of it. I have seen it demonstrated often enough before my own eyes. What I argue for is the perfect right of those who have "borne the heat and burden of the day" to have a time of freedom from carrying the responsibilities of community and church.

Some of my acquaintances have spoken quite disdainfully of being stripped of their powers and "turned out to pasture" like old worn-out horses. I understand the analogy, but I have another mental picture as well. I remember the horses in my father's pasture, two of them in the shade of a willow tree, standing head to tail in order to maximize the effectiveness of their rhythmic tail switching. They were the perfect picture of contentment. Do I hear the protest, "I am not a horse!"

How then do people whose public responsibilities have been laid aside and whose physical capacities may be diminished spend their time in order to avoid boredom?

Many people find in retirement opportunities for travel which they never had before. Esther and I found in our several trips to Europe—one to the Holy Land and other parts of the Middle East—occasions for enjoyment and for continued growth and appreciation of our Judeo-Christian heritage. We went to Alaska and found it not only the land of the midnight sun but the land of the golden-agers as well. I am sure senior citizens have carried more gold into Alaska than the sourdoughs ever took out. My only advice to those who cherish the dream of travel abroad, "Don't put it off too long." As we grow older, health more uncertain and vigor declining, travel becomes less easy and less enjoyable.

Don't think I left you behind because you don't have the money or the physical stamina for a trip to Alaska or the Middle East or even a three-week bus tour to the Rockies. In every community are the makings of one-day or overnight trips. What do you like? Museums, historical sights, battlefields, old mansions, famous churches or cathedrals, caves, waterfalls, state or national parks? You name it, and it will probably be available.

Perhaps you have some personal reason for choosing a particular site. I wanted to visit the mansion of a particular coal king of yesterday because it bore my name—Linden Hall. I particularly enjoyed visiting the birthplace, near Marlinton, West Virginia, of the writer Pearl Buck, because on my mother's side of the family, we claim Pearl Buck as a distant cousin. Whatever the reasons, there will be something to enjoy. For Esther and me, a day trip into the hills of West Virginia with no particular destination in mind is just ideal. If perchance we don't make it back home in one day, we look for a motel when the sun goes down.

Another whole area of social activity for seniors is the playing of table games. A way to spend winter evenings with a few friends, it provides pleasant conversation and more or less serious competition of wits or luck. Table games may be a life saver where larger crowds happen to be together, affording a way to break the group into smaller and more intimate units.

The variety of games is endless—all the card games, Checkers, Dominoes, Scrabble, Trivia, Monopoly and all the games of chance that begin with shaking out the dice. Many of these games do serve to keep our wits sharpened so that our aging brainpower does not diminish by neglect. Others depend on chance and afford no particular challenge to brainpower.

I salute table games but, at the same time, confess that most of them have not been very attractive to me. When somebody mentions Scrabble, I am likely to scramble. I spent too much of my life pushing words around for a living, and to do so now is not exactly my idea of relaxation. Strangely enough, I am more attracted by the solitary exercise of doing the *Reader's Digest* "It pays to increase your word power" page. I seldom do it in competition—just brag a bit to my wife when I make an exceptionally good score.

My negative remarks about table games afford me the chance to say I do not expect anyone to like everything suggested in this chapter, and I also do not expect everyone to like the same things—that would be a bit tragic. Whether in travels, hobbies or leisure pursuits, we should all be discriminating, doing what we like best, what most relaxes and fulfills us and what makes us and those around us most happy.

Many older persons simply need company—a group with which to identify. In my end of town a loosely-organized club has formed. By their own designation, duly posted on their own turf, the "The Old Bones Club" is "Afflicted with bad memory, blessed with good humor." Not bad for a start! Every summer afternoon they play shuffleboard for a couple of hours. In winter they move to the basement of a nearby college dorm to play pool. Should someone want them for something else during their regularly scheduled meeting, they do not hesitate to say, "Sorry, I have another appointment." I have frequently been invited to join. Other more urgent things have so far required my attention, but I am keeping my options open. I may still join because I recognize how meaningful the relationship is. It provides regular social contact, and the men definitely are a support group to one another while having fun.

Doubtless, the world's oldest ritual of social interaction and cementing the obligations of friendship and support is simply eating together. In ancient cultures, it symbolized a moral obligation far beyond what we usually give it in modern America. One did not lift a hand against the individual with whom one had broken bread.

In most families, having guests and being guests is a large part of social life and the solidifying of family relationships. In the older years when children and grandchildren are scattered, when our familiar friends are dropping out one by one, the intimate fellowship of eating together becomes more and more important. It may be two or three men around a table in the local cafe with a cup of coffee and a doughnut. It may be two or three women in an apartment with a cup of tea and cookies. Perhaps we meet on a regular basis. In any case, there is no hurry.

Larger groups may plan restaurant meals together, once a week or once a month, designed purely for fellowship and mutual encouragement. Other groups may want to add Bible study and prayer to the fellowship. People who have common backgrounds in previous professional or business interests may meet regularly to keep abreast of their familiar world. Other groups may choose the intellectual stimulation of a new book or an agreed-upon discussion topic.

I especially want to say a word to all retirees about the joy and challenge of going to senior retreats. Most church camps, many fraternal organizations, many state recreational or human services departments have one or more senior weeks in their yearly schedules. Esther and I have been going to the Laurelville Mennonite Center's senior week for the past eight years. A high point of our year, a great place to meet old friends and make new ones, a source of intellectual challenge and stimulation, it is just a great place to relax and have fun. Try it!

When You Are Housebound

Finally, how can people who no longer have private transportation, who may be housebound or who are living in a retirement complex make time a matter of anticipation rather than a drag?

I should say I live nextdoor to Virginia Mennonite Retirement Center (VMRC) with its three or four stages of retired living. I am continually amazed at the activities provided for the VMRC campus—crafts, music, films, lectures, talent opportunities and off-campus trips. I am grateful. But what actual service opportunities exist for those among us who are less mobile?

First, there are telephone opportunities. Churches or social agencies often set up telephone watches where people are called, once or twice a day, to check on their well-being and to provide social contact. The designated caller must take some initiative and responsibility and is rewarded with a sense of having done something significant.

Second, whatever happened to the art of letter writing? Our modern way of life and communicating seem to have made it almost obsolete. There is still a real ministry in letter writing for those who are willing to take the time and effort. I don't mean long letters necessarily but notes of appreciation, encouragement, sympathy or even just a cheerful greeting.

Third, a profound need for the ministry of prayer exists. Prayer is hard work and requires time and devotion. I have known a few individuals who, in their older years, became great prayer warriors. Or, perhaps, they continued to be prayer warriors, and the fruits of their ministry simply became more openly apparent. The church and the world need such volunteers.

Don't worry, as long as you live, you will have something significant to do if you are willing to do it.

8. Coping with Loneliness

By the rivers of Babylon, there we sat down,
yea, we wept when we remembered Zion.

(Ps. 137:1)

Overcoming loneliness
is like trying
to have the last word
with an echo.

Soon after I began working with the Older Adults Ministries in my church conference, our committee did a survey of the over-sixty members in our congregations. We wanted to know what they needed and how they felt about their relationships to their family, their church and their community. There were questions about living arrangements, family relations, church and community activities and personal feelings. Of course, we included a question about loneliness. I had always heard that loneliness was one of the major problems plaguing the elderly. When the questionnaires came back, there were relatively few persons who admitted that loneliness was a problem in their lives.

I was delighted. My first conclusion was that our church and our Christian families were taking care of the elderly among them in such a way that they felt accepted and wanted. Consequently, they did not experience loneliness. Then I heard from Ann Bender. She works with both a community-based agency serving the elderly and several church agencies, and she warned, "Now don't take all that at face value. People do not like to admit they are lonely. They may feel to admit loneliness is to acknowledge failure on their part or to put fault on someone else." I have come to accept Ann's analysis.

The Composition of Loneliness

Webster defines lonely as being without company, cut off from others, sad from being alone. Actually, loneliness carries many more overtones than simply being without human company. Loneliness can be complicated and accentuated by feelings of estrangement, rejection, vulnerability, uselessness or fear.

We frequently attribute loneliness to objects or places. The lonely land is one not inhabited by humans. The lonely little house on the prairie has nothing to do with the house itself but with the feelings of the one who looks at it or perhaps the memories of one who spent long days there without human company, without communication (no telephone, no letters), or perhaps in fear of what might happen in such a situation.

Even being in the presence of people, many people, does not ensure that a person will not be lonely. Often people are lonely in large cities. They may walk the streets with thousands, rub elbows with them in stores, sit with them in theaters and restaurants, yet they are lonely. They do not know these people by name. They are not free to share with them their own feelings, sorrows and joys. They remain alone. When these people become old, they may be afraid to venture out on the streets because of a very real fear of bodily harm. They barricade themselves in their apartments and remain alone in body, mind and spirit.

They tell me many people in large cities are unfriendly. I think, rather, they are afraid. If they reveal themselves, a stranger may take advantage of them—rip them off. So both the visitor and the native learn to be wary of one another.

As a young man, working for a poultry equipment firm, I was sent to Long Island on a service call. I had a bit of difficulty locating my client. Finally, I drove into a poultry yard where I saw a man outside and asked him if he knew Mr. So-and-so. He shrugged his shoulders, gave me the "why should I know" look and shook his head. Just then I noticed a building scarcely a hundred yards away, on top of which I recognized some of our equipment. "Who lives over there?" I asked, pointing. The results were the same, a shrug and the admission that he did not know. I could not believe it. However, with a better acquaintance, I have found that once this mutual fear and distrust can be laid aside, people in large cities are as friendly as anyone else.

I am aware from my studies that people in many primitive tribes are quite reluctant to give their names to a stranger. Upon a first meeting, the individual often gives a fictitious name. The underlying idea is that when someone knows your name, they obtain a certain power over you.

I remember the story of Hagar when she fled from her mistress, Sarah. The angel of the Lord intercepted her, calling her by name and telling her to return. Hagar was amazed that the Lord knew her name. She called the place Beer Lahai Roi—the well of the one who lives and sees me.

I feel the basic ingredient of loneliness is just this sense of estrangement and alienation. When Adam had finished surveying and naming all of the creatures God brought before him, he realized no creature corresponded exactly to himself. Adam was lonely. So God created woman, using a rib out of Adam's side. Adam was at union with his own, at peace with himself and no longer lonely.

Loneliness as Estrangement

Alas! This state of perfect harmony did not long continue. Enter the experience of rebellion and sin. First of all came the estrangement from God. Adam blamed his wife, and the estrangement of humanity from itself began. Adam and Eve were driven from the Garden, and humankind was estranged from creation as well. God immediately set about working out a plan by which we could be restored to relationship and fellowship with our Creator. This is our greatest hope and, today, our greatest help for coping with the loneliness brought about by the estrangement of sin.

The loneliness of estrangement is amply demonstrated in Scripture, in secular literature, in history and in our struggle with nature. Our estrangement from each other was soon demonstrated in Cain's murder of Abel. When the consequences of his deed were outlined, Cain cried out in lonely agony, "My punishment is greater than I can bear! Surely you have driven me out this day from the face of the ground. I shall be hidden from your face; I shall be a fugitive and a vagabond on the earth" (Gen. 4:14). We are told that Cain went out from the presence of the Lord and dwelt in the land of Nod—the land of wandering.

Estrangement from Creation

Sociologists and psychologists often speak of a "cosmic loneliness" experienced even in the presence of or, at least, availability of human company. This is that vague, or maybe not so vague, feeling of estrangement from the creation itself.

Did you ever sit outdoors on a summer night and hear frogs croaking in the distance or crickets chirping in a nearby meadow or a hoot owl calling from the mountainside? How did it make you feel? Most people say it creates a sense of loneliness. I have never heard coyotes howl at night, but I am told it provokes a lonely, mournful sensation.

From my high school days I remember several lines from Henry W. Longfellow's poem, "My Lost Youth." Note that title! The lines themselves are from an old Lapland nuptial song.

> For a boy's will is the wind's will,
> And the thoughts of youth are long, long thoughts.[1]

It is apparent that feelings of loneliness are not particular to old age. In that connection, I recall several things that stirred those long and lonely thoughts in my own youthful mind. I remember one winter day as I sat on the sunny side of a fodder shock while the wind blew overhead. My heart was in a sort of tug-of-war between the cozy warmth of the sun-warmed corn leaves and the chill of the wind blowing from faraway places.

Also when I was a boy, our chickens weren't always confined to their houses but ran loose in the farmyard. Sometimes on a quiet afternoon, one of the family roosters would stand in the barn lot and crow a long bugle call which definitely had a different pitch than he used among the hens in early morning. Soon a rooster would answer him from the farm to our west. Presently, a rooster from the farm to the north would join in. What these roosters were communicating I don't know, but their ringing, far-reaching sound stirred in me those long thoughts of faraway places and unfulfilled dreams.

I know very little of the basic underlying theology of the

native American Indian religion. One thing, however, that has impressed me is its fundamental respect and reverence for nature, for the created world and all its inhabitants. That caring reverence seems largely lost from the sensitivities of industrialized Western people. I see in it not only the search to find the Creator, but also the desire to be restored in harmony to the creation itself.

Loss of Supporting Peers

Enough of "cosmic loneliness." We can do nothing about it except perhaps try to understand it. I consider the basic ingredient of loneliness to be a sense of estrangement—from God, from our fellows and from creation. While the loneliness produced by this estrangement is by no means confined to old age, it is likely to be intensified in the experience of aging and to begin producing distress, even suffering.

In older years, the sources of loneliness multiply. There are so many changes, so many losses, which break the well-worn patterns of life. It is easy to develop the feeling of having lost contact. I heard an elderly bishop tell a story from his childhood. His father was going to town and promised to take the boy along. He was instructed to wait by the yard gate until his father had hitched the horse to the spring wagon. The father got everything ready and then, in his own preoccupation, drove off to town, leaving the boy standing forlorn and forsaken by the gate. Many older people feel that life has treated them just that way.

The primary loss facing many elderly people is the loss of a spouse. The "life events scale" developed by psychiatrist, Dr. Thomas A. Holmes, and designed to measure the psychological stress factors caused by various life events rates the loss of a spouse at 100. By comparison, the second most stressful life event, divorce, is rated 73. All others noted on the chart range from 65 downward.[2] The loss of a spouse breaks years of companionship, understanding, support and sharing that leaves life empty and in disarray. The long-term effect of this loss is likely to be a great sense of loneliness, a longing for something which cannot be restored. For those who have not been married, a comparable loss may be the death of a sibling or close friend with whom one has had living quarters or spiritual and emotional intimacy and support.

In these experiences, the differences between men and women are worth noting. The Bible indicates that woman is the "weaker vessel." I accept it in its context, but I will refrain from any theological discussion as to wherein that relative strength and weakness lies. Present-day statistics show that women live longer than men by about four years, beginning at birth. In 1990, for those reaching sixty-five, males had a life expectancy of 15.3 years and females of 19.0 years. Widows outnumbered widowers by five to one, due in part to the fact that men were more likely to remarry than women.[3]

Psychologists agree that women are better able to cope with the loss of a spouse than are men. Many men have traditionally not been adept at cooking, housekeeping and taking care of their own health. Women are more likely to pick up the business and financial skills necessary for survival. Men are less able to pick up the necessary household and health skills. Women are more adept at putting life together again than are men. This, in part, may explain why men are more likely to remarry. When the loss of a spouse turns into a long haul, it is one of the major sources of loneliness.

Aside from the loss of a spouse, the loss of other family members breaks the pattern of our lives and leaves us at loose ends. Siblings always have some special relationship. They may drift apart while each is busy raising his or her own family and making a living. It has been interesting to me to see how, after retirement, these siblings often draw together again. They visit, have meals together and reminisce about old times. When these sibling groups are broken by death, there is a great sense of loss. A piece of life is gone which cannot be replaced. Their going leaves for us, in the words of Edwin Markham, "a lonely place against the sky."[4]

Another acute producer of loneliness and the sense of being forgotten for older persons is separation from their own children. Business, professional and church assignments scatter most families across the country and overseas as well. Many parents do not see their children and grandchildren more than a couple of times a year and sometimes not for several years. More than one parent facing the prospect of moving to a retirement home or nursing care facility has said bitterly, "I took care of my children when they were little. I thought they would take care of me when I was old." The complaint may, or may not, be justified, but that does not necessarily relieve the feeling of abandonment and loneliness. When children live within reasonable visiting distance and still do not visit, an added sense of bitterness often results.

People who live to a more advanced age will see their friends pass on one by one. Those who can share their remembrances of good days gone by or hard times endured together, those who understand and share their ideas, will become fewer and fewer. If one is not aggressive in cultivating new acquaintances along the way, this dropping off of old friends can leave one more and more isolated and lonely.

Separation from Familiar Things

The physical changes which come with growing older can often be the source of sad and lonely feelings. The big old house where the family grew up, where the children played and perhaps left some of their childhood possessions, may no longer be practical. It may be too much for an elderly couple to keep up and so may need to be sold. No matter how practical the decision may be, parting with the physical location and physical objects which are reminders, recollections and prompters of our fondest memories undoubtedly will generate some trauma.

Down-scaling the size of living quarters always means sorting out and discarding some of our possessions. Some of us will go through this sorting process more than once, moving from a big house to a small one to an apartment to a retirement facility and eventually even to a nursing home. Somewhere along the line, it becomes a matter not only of giving up furniture and appliances but of giving up keepsakes as well—heirlooms, family pictures and sentimental gifts. Naturally, this is more difficult for some than for others. The separation from familiar places and things can be a source of extreme loneliness to some individuals.

Negative Memories and Positive Faith
Another cause of loneliness among the elderly is too much time. They have too much time to think, and they do it with negative results. Now let's look at this one carefully. Earlier I said that I believe the elderly are entitled to leisure time; time to reminisce and put things together. But some people are prone to negative thinking. They remember all the hurts and disappointments of life, all the people who have wronged or slighted them in any way. Or they zero in on the hurts they have experienced within their own family, the real or imagined unfairness of siblings, the real or imagined partiality of parents to a brother or sister. Anyone who wishes to dwell on life's unfairness will have plenty of material to work on. Remember, life may not be fair. Only God is never unfair toward His children.

Another trick the elderly sometimes play on themselves is to dwell on their own real or imagined failures. Particularly, they blame themselves if their children turned out to be a disappointment, or if some unfortunate decision or action of their own brought shame or suffering on those whom they loved and to whom they really meant to do good. Dwelling on such things can produce an insufferable load of guilt and alienation.

A few years ago, certain psychologists of the youth cult gave the current generation of parents a bad time. According to these apologists of youth, no one under thirty was to blame for anything—they were simply the products of a generation of parents whose misguided values had set the children on a false and aimless course of greed and self-interest. Some of us sensitive souls really suffered under that accusation. One day I had a saving thought, "If the present generation of parents is responsible for the warped values of the upcoming generation, then what about us? Can we help it if we are what we are? Are we not also blameless because of the misguided impressions received from our parents?" Of course, that could go on in infinite regress until we reach poor old Grandpa Adam who has nowhere to hide. Little is gained from agonizing over the real or imaginary failures which have marked our life's journey. And yet, the culture in which we live and even sometimes the church have been pretty adept at laying guilt trips on us. All this simply multiplies our sense of failure, estrangement and loneliness, prone to increase with the years. Is there a balm for the weary and lonely spirit?

It is my own feeling and the witness of many others that personal faith in Jesus Christ is our greatest bulwark against any and all the forces that batter us in life, whether we are young, middle-aged or old. We are all made up differently—physically, emotionally and psychologically. We will differ in the way and to the degree in which we apprehend the presence of Christ with us in daily life. It is normal to anticipate that as we mature in years, we also mature in faith. However, this does not guarantee that when we reach retirement, our struggles are over. Rather, most of us will have significant processing and adjusting to do. I will say again that the mature Christian faith is our greatest hedge against loneliness and anxiety.

In the words from the chorus of an old song, the Christian is promised the presence of Jesus.

> No, never alone,
> No, never alone!
> He promised never to leave me,
> Never to leave me alone.[5]

Many persons attest to the reality of Jesus' daily presence. Older persons often struggle with the sense of being no longer useful. When they cannot perform the tasks by which they served their family and community, they tend to lose their sense of worth, their self-esteem. Christian faith assures us we are persons of worth in God's sight. Christ died for us. God has prepared for us a place in Heaven. Our life here on earth was in His plan and for His glory. We have reason to be cheerful and confident.

Keep Busy

Loneliness may be out-maneuvered with activity. When we are busy with our hands or our minds, there is no room to brood over things we have been pushed out of, people who have left us behind or the incidental fact that no one visited us today. The human body and the human mind are both designed for activity, and with it many things are kept in focus. Without activity, things tend to come unglued. "Idleness is the devil's workshop," we say to young people whose minds may be easily enticed to evil. To the elderly, enforced idleness may well be the devil's prison house, plunging us into loneliness and discouragement.

It used to be the custom at Eastern Mennonite College to give retirees a finely-crafted rocking chair. When I received my chair in a public ceremony, I remarked tongue-in-cheek, "Well, this chair will have a good home; it won't need to work hard." And that was about right. I cherish it as a remembrance but seldom use it simply for leisure. Esther was even more astute. She turned down the rocking chair for a more practical, if less enduring, piece of technological equipment.

Do not suppose it is only the residents of retirement homes who are plagued with idleness. The one who, for lack of imagination to find more fruitful activity, spends his or her hours watching television is doomed to a lonely existence. For the person with no hobby, the morning paper furnishes only a brief oasis in an otherwise long and barren day.

According to a current story, when the great modern Egyptian President Nassar died and was banished to the land of the Shades, he was visited one day by the ancient King Tut, who found Nassar watching television. "This is not fair," raged King Tut. "You have this lively entertainment all day long; I have nothing but the hieroglyphics on the walls of my dreary tomb."

"But you don't understand," protested Nassar. "This is my punishment; it was for my sins I have been condemned to watch this idiot box for a thousand years."

A woodworking shop occupies the hands, requires some creativity and demands attention. Needlework likewise occupies the hands, demands attention and nourishes thoughts of the one for whom the piece may be intended. Writing one's own life story can occupy a lot of time and certainly encourages a lot of wholesome reflection on life's meaning, purposes and achievements. The children and grandchildren will thank us for our efforts.

To combat loneliness, cultivate people. Our most common notion of the cause of loneliness in the first place is the absence of company, the lack of someone to talk with. While this is not altogether true, or at least the whole story, it is very basic. We are social creatures. People, more than any other of God's creation, have the power of communication, the power to comfort, to stimulate and to challenge one another with words. By the power of abstract thinking, we share ideas, develop society and perceive ourselves as a part of history. We need each other. Every normal person loves company.

It is important that we cultivate the art of making friends throughout life. Sometimes people fail to replace the friends they lose along the way and find themselves as older persons with only a small circle of intimate acquaintances. I really can't say if it is more difficult to make friends when we become older. Certainly we lose some of the spontaneity of children and need to guard against becoming so set in our ways that we may fend off our would-be friends. On the other hand, the experiences of life may mellow us and condition us to reach out readily and with understanding to those about us.

Nothing boosts our sense of self-worth and drives away loneliness more quickly than doing something for someone in need. When you feel sorry for yourself, find someone for whom to do a favor. It may be only a word of encouragement and kindness, some physical assistance, an appropriate gift. When you make the day brighter for someone else, you do it for yourself as well. One of the old Greek recipes for dealing with tragedy suggested remembering there were others whose condition was worse than one's own. Carried to its ultimate conclusion, this could conceivably be true of all but one person in the world at any given time. Think about that. This may be a rather backhanded way of consoling ourselves in our misfortunes. It does serve to put us on notice that there should be no difficulty in finding someone on whom we can bestow a favor whether we consider their situation better or worse than our own.

Do You Talk to Your Flowers?

Not to be forgotten among the assuagers of loneliness are pets. They can be particularly helpful to persons who must live alone. Lately pets have come to be recognized as having definite therapeutic powers for those who are confined to nursing homes or other institutions. Our daughter works in a psychiatric hospital. One of the "resident doctors" is George, a nondescript, but friendly, cat.

I must confess I once thought people who talked to dogs, cats or birds, as though they were human, were just a bit unusual. Having lived long enough to observe the relationship between persons, who might otherwise have been lonely, and their pets, I have changed my mind. These pets, being alive, can respond in interesting, almost personal, ways to their owner-companions. Certainly, talking to a cat does not appear nearly so stupid as talking to oneself. Taking care of a pet can be time-filling and entertaining. Most important, it provides company.

Should a live pet be impossible, indoor flowers and plants provide an outlet for many persons. To feed the aesthetic sensibilities which all of us possess enlarges our lives and increases joy. To deny the aesthetic part of our nature decreases our personalities and may even increase the sense of loneliness and the interminable nature of time. Both pets and plants give us something to share with others. They provide pleasant bits of conversation with friends.

When all else fails, some people talk to their plants. Many

botanists agree that it is neither stupid nor futile. Some scientists feel they have adequately documented that plants respond to the kindly treatment represented by the talking of their caretakers. I am sure the caretakers respond to the encouragement given to them ever so silently by their plants.

It's Your Move

Finally, the quality of our own life and spirit is pretty much up to us as individuals. We can determine to be cheerful in the face of what life gives us, or we can complain, worry and fret about every unpleasant circumstance. We can easily promote our own loneliness by making ourselves unpleasant company. I have heard attributed to several well-known figures the saying, "Most people are just about as happy as they make up their minds to be." I don't know who said it first, but the saying is worth repeating. I wouldn't mind if it were attributed to me!

Being a Christian does not necessarily make people kind and cheerful, but it certainly ought to help. The little girl who prayed, "God, please make all the bad people good and all the good people nice," had certainly caught the correct idea. Christian faith and a cheerful spirit ought to go hand-in-hand. No one should be so naive as to think that life is always fair. There will be misunderstandings, misfortune, rebuff and failure. It is what happens after the rebuff or misfortune that counts. My readers have probably all heard the old saying about ulcers. "Ulcers are not the result of what you eat but what eats you." Each one of us will determine the way in which we respond to others' behavior. We can nurture anger and carry a grudge, or we can accept the rebuff, forgive from the heart and concentrate on the good things of life.

Somewhere I read that no one can be offended unless they are willing to be—that is, unless they personally own the offense. I heard the story, too, of a Christian gentleman who was furiously maligned by a colleague. He took it calmly and made no reply. A friend was more upset and demanded, "Why did you let him get by with that? Why didn't you tell him off?" Replied the gentleman quietly, "I never pick up things that don't belong to me."

A friend of mine told the story of a traveler who came to the railroad dining car with the intention of ordering a steak for his dinner. When he found there was no steak on the menu, he flew into a rage and began to abuse the waiter. The steward came and tried to pacify the irate diner. "We will soon be coming to Cleveland where we have a rather long stop. I will send out and get you a steak," promised the steward.

"Never mind," roared the diner, "I would rather be mad." In the final analysis, it is rather heartening to know that our ultimate happiness or unhappiness is pretty much in our own hands rather than at the disposal of others.

After You've Made the Move

In this book I have focused primarily on retirement and beyond. A time of life when loneliness caused by the lack of contact with familiar persons is most likely to develop, it begins with leaving the workplace. At retirement people often also change their place of residence, sometimes to a new community where an entirely new circle of friends must be built. At this time families are likely to be scattered, and death has begun to take an increasing toll of lifelong friends and family.

So long as we are fully mobile, the responsibility of a satisfying number of human contacts lies primarily with us. We can invite company into our own house, visit family or friends, join social clubs or initiate support groups of new friends. Usually the possibilities of social contact lie as close as our telephone.

It is when people lose mobility that the situation becomes more trying. When individuals no longer have personal transportation, when they are confined to their own house or apartment or when they become residents of a retirement facility or nursing home, the situation is different. These people become dependent on other people coming to them, and sometimes they have just reason for their feelings of loneliness and abandonment.

In my twenty-five years as an overseer, the complaint I heard most often against ministers was this, "My pastor doesn't come to see me." Now I suspect that many times the accusation was not justified. Perhaps sometimes it was. The same accusation is lodged against children. The days get long in an institution, and it is easy to say, "My children don't visit me." I suspect in most cases if the children visited twice as often, it would make very little difference in the loneliness of the parents or other older relatives. I offer some advice for all parties in these situations.

To pastors, I emphasize the importance of arranging regular visitation for all the elderly in the congregation and especially for those who are shut in. It does not always need to be the pastor but someone representing the care of the congregation. To those who have elderly parents or other older relatives, the most precious gift you can bring to them is the gift of your own presence. It is more important to be frequent than to be long.

Now to all retirees, whether housebound or still active, I say it is up to us to take the primary responsibility for our own good cheer and happiness. Rejoice in the good memories you have of life. Rejoice in the good health and accomplishments of your children. Remember how busy and full of activity life was when you were the present age of your children.

Of course, I know how parents feel about wanting to see

their children and grandchildren. Esther and I have three children. One lives 600 miles away, so we know we must be content with seeing his family once or twice a year. Our daughter is 200 miles away, so it is a few weekends a year, definitely not a Sunday afternoon visit. Fortunately for us, the other son with his wife and two children is only 20 miles away. We see each other every few weeks, at our house or theirs, and it is great.

Must I confess that sometimes on a Sunday afternoon, I begin to think, "Now why couldn't they come to see us today?" I can usually set those thoughts under control by remembering the program under which we lived while those children were growing up and how often we did, or didn't, visit our own parents in those days. So I say again, to myself and all my elderly compatriots, "Don't expect too much of your grown children. Keep busy according to your strength and circumstances. Rediscover the ancient springs of joy in your own heart. 'A cheerful heart is good medicine'" (Proverbs 17:22a, NIV).

9. A Few Last Minute Things

Whatever your hand finds to do, do it with your might;
for there is no work, or device, or knowledge, or wisdom
in the grave, where you are going.

Making both ends meet is a losing game
—a baby can put its toes in its mouth,
an old man can scarcely
tie his shoes.

As a preacher I have long nurtured an obsession with getting to church on time, which being interpreted means at least twenty or thirty minutes ahead of scheduled beginning. My long-suffering wife has had to put up all these years with my regular Sunday morning plea, "It's time to go; aren't you about ready?"

Her standard and very logical reply has been, "Now, you must remember, there are always a few last-minute things to be done."

To which I would sometimes reply with equal logic, "Yes,

but can't those last minute things be pushed up a little with a bit of planning?"

Making a Will

Life is a bit like that. There are some last minute things which ought not to be put off until the "last minute." One of the most important is preparing a will. With all the information passed out by church groups, financial institutions and community organizations, it would seem no one would neglect making a will. That is not the case, however. Many of us put off making wills because putting it off is easier than doing it. Everybody has time, but many people never take time for a task which demands such sober thought.

Some people have the idea that because their estate is small and their possessions meager, they do not need a will. A will, according to them, is for persons of wealth and large possessions. Wrong! If you have anything which you wish someone specific to have after you are gone, if you wish your spouse and children to have their interests in whatever you possess, little or much, properly safeguarded, then you need a will. If you have no will, the state will take over the distribution of your estate. It will cost money, and your family, especially your spouse, may suffer unjustly and unnecessarily.

Some of us entertain the notion that making a will should be done after we get older. We have made our fortune, and nothing is likely to change. This, too, is a mistake. While children are small, they, more than ever, need to have their interests protected. A young widow's needs may be seriously jeopardized when there is no will. Most families will normally have occasion to update their wills as the years go by and family and financial circumstances change.

Then, there are those persons who have a sort of morbid fear of dealing with anything they perceive as being connected with death. For them, to make provision for the disposition of affairs at death invites disaster. Nonsense, of course, but like any other phobia, it may be very real. Such an idea often indicates some other disorientation in their lives for which counseling with a pastor or psychologist may be helpful.

When preparing a will, it is wise to consult a lawyer. A personal or family attorney will usually provide such service for a modest fee. Handwritten wills, properly signed, are also still considered valid. However, given the intricacies of legal language which have developed over the years, most laymen in the field are hardly prepared to tie all the threads and close all the loopholes with correct legal terminology. One should also probably beware of the "write your own will" kits which are advertised for a few dollars. While they may contain helpful information for preparing a handwritten will, one cannot simply fill in the blanks in a prepared document. Such a paper does not constitute a valid will. The best to hope for from a do-it-yourself kit are instructions for a complete and separate writing of a personal will. The services of an attorney are better and possibly even cheaper in the end.

Powers of Attorney

A second document, now considered just as important, provides for power of attorney. In case of your disability or incapacity for any reason, someone is duly authorized to conduct your financial affairs. Again, it may be prepared by an attorney for a reasonable fee. Should you neglect it until incapacitation, your family will need a court order to establish power of attorney. This is certain to add expense and stress. Taking care of such matters before illness lessens the strain on your family and is a great kindness to them and anyone else involved. Be sure to indicate the time and circumstances under which a power of attorney document is activated.

It should be noted there are several different powers of attorney. A simple power of attorney authorizes another person to carry on your financial affairs at your direction, or in your absence, but does not empower such a person to manage your finances if you become incapacitated.

For authorization to manage affairs in cases of incapacitation, the designated person needs durable power of attorney. A document giving durable power of attorney should somehow indicate what type of authorization is being given, most likely a clause stating "this power of attorney shall not terminate upon my disability."

More recently, something called medical power of attorney has been developed which designates someone to have power to determine what medical procedures may or may not be taken in case of illness or injury so severe that the ill or injured person cannot make decisions.

Be very careful whom you nominate as executor of your will and be especially careful to whom you give power of attorney. Once activated, power of attorney gives broad authority to the individual to do business with your money, not only to pay bills but to buy and sell property and to make investments. It provides opportunity for anyone not strictly honest to direct or misdirect funds to their own personal interest. Some people will feel more comfortable naming a bank to manage their financial affairs. This will likely be more expensive, and the world being what it is, even banks have been known to misuse and deplete the funds entrusted to them.

Many persons name one of their children to administer their estate and to have power of attorney. When no children are available, a close and trusted relative should be chosen. Blessed is the family where this can be done with perfect love and confidence. Unfortunately, again, there are times when this may not be the wise choice.

However, I am not an expert on these matters. The obser-vations and suggestions which I have listed do not result from an exhaustive study of the laws governing wills, estate distri-bution, estate taxes, powers of attorney and trusts. They grow out of a lifetime of observation and consultation with my own legal and financial counselors. My counselors always warn me that laws governing these matters are constantly changing and they vary widely from state to state. If the above discus-sion raises any questions, I recommend seeing some properly-informed person—your lawyer or accountant—and determining for certain the laws in your state of residence.

At retirement, a change of residence frequently occurs, sometimes a move to another state. When such is the case, it is wise to be sure all your legal papers conform to the laws in the new state of residence. These moves accompanying retire-ment, even though they may not be out of state, often disrupt familiar support systems. You may need to change doctors or leave behind a lawyer and a dentist. It is wise to reestablish a support system in the new place before emergencies arise. Everyone needs a doctor whom they trust, and this medical network should include access to a hospital. Everyone also needs a dentist, a lawyer, a financial counselor and, surely, a pastor in whom he or she has confidence. Further, it helps to know the location of other community services, particularly those offering assistance to the elderly.

Living Will and Medical Power of Attorney

Today many people also prepare living wills. Basically, this document informs family and medical personnel not to pro-long life by artificial and heroic means in case of terminal illness when death is imminent and hope of effectual recovery is gone. Given the present state of medical science, one may be kept physically alive even after any prospect of pleasure or usefulness in life are gone. Many people consider this artificial prolonging of life an insult to personhood, even an infringement on the intentions of the Creator. The living will allows an individual to assert his or her right to die with dignity. Should the person be unconscious or otherwise unable to indicate a decision, it becomes the responsibility of the family and physician to see that the dying one's desires are fulfilled.

The living will has been regarded with a great deal of apprehension by the medical profession and the courts. Its validity has been discussed by a number of state legislative bodies, but no uniform legal policy has yet been written. A number of bitter court battles have been fought over the rights of parents or family—with or without the living will—to order the removal of artificial life support systems. While not yet considered a fully legal document, both the medical and legal professions recognize a living will more and more often as representing the wishes of the ill or injured person.

We may learn one important thing from recent legal battles. If a living will is to be honored, it must be fully in place as the expressed wish of its framer before the time of crisis arises. Since more and more of us feel it has a valid place in the world of medical science, it becomes another one of those last minute things that need to be done before the "last minute" arrives. However, the matter needs to be thought through carefully. Some persons hesitate to put this burden of responsibility on their families. Yet in a time of crisis, families may be left to wish their loved one had spoken specifically.

Much has been happening recently to clarify the legal status and the practical use of both the living will and the medical power of attorney. In 1990 Congress passed the Patient Self-Determination Act. It went into effect in 1992 and requires hospitals and other health care institutions to tell patients upon admission about their rights under their own state law to make decisions about medical care, their right to accept or refuse medical treatment and their right to give advance directives. For example, the Virginia legislature enacted the Virginia Natural Death Act in 1983. It was not too vigorously promoted until the Congressional action became effective.

Both the living will and the medical power of attorney must be signed by two witnesses who are not blood relatives or beneficiaries of your estate. In some states the power of attorney must also be notarized. The services of a lawyer are not required. Also, neither of these documents becomes effective without the written statement of a physician and, in many cases, the signatures of at least two medical personnel.

How Living Wills and Medical Powers of Attorney Are Used

No one is required to write personal advance directives in a living will. However, if you have such a document—indicating whether or not you wish to be put on life support should the need arise—the hospital will want a copy for the file. If you have none, you will be given a brochure and, likely, forms which you may fill out for both living will and medical power of attorney. Obviously, the emergency room of a hospital is not the ideal setting for filling out such documents.

Each state has, or soon will have, its own laws governing the use of advance directives. In making such provision, be sure to follow the codes of your home state. Should you change your residence—perhaps move to a retirement home in another state—be sure to update your documents to comply with your new state of residence.

Not all states have settled the legal status of the living will, but the current emphasis on advance directives will certainly hasten this procedure. The standardization of state codes does much to relieve hospitals and doctors of the old fear of lawsuits, hanging constantly over their heads.

The most recent provision written into some state codes has to do with the administration of emergency medical services. Persons who have a terminal illness but reside at home may secure from their physician a statement which entitles them to a DNR (do not resusitate) order. Worn on their person, it tells either emergency or hospital personnel not to employ the usual measures to restore breathing or heartbeat.

These provisions are relatively new. In the days of our parents and grandparents, medical science had not progressed to the point where the artificial prolonging of physical life was a question which needed to be faced, nor were the costs of final medical care likely to produce a family financial crisis. Today it is different.

I must consider what I owe myself, my family and my community by making provision for the closure of my personal affairs related to final medical services. Admittedly, it is one of those things which most people would rather not deal with forthrightly. Our local older adults services program has been promoting advance directives in recent months. Most people admit it is a good idea. They readily take our literature, but many are slow to finalize these documents and a few are actually fearful.

I believe it is a matter of maturity to make closure of personal affairs and to face the issue. Families should talk it over, primarily because it is hardly fair to leave these things to loved ones to decide in a time of crisis without any indication of our own wishes. To safeguard ourselves and everyone concerned, our directives must be written down before a time of crisis comes.

Sad as it may sound, the cost of dying has become a major consideration. The final few months of a terminal illness, spent in semi-consciousness at the end of an array of tubes and needles, may easily cost more than a long lifetime of medical expenses. A family may become impoverished simply because the dying process of a loved one has been futilely prolonged.

Perhaps you planned to leave the proceeds of your estate to your children and to the church or some other charity. Do you want that all wiped out by one last bit of extraordinary care which hospitals are duty-bound to give you unless you have indicated otherwise?

Your own spiritual orientation will determine your attitude toward death. For the Christian its terror is taken away. In fact, whether it is possible to harmonize artificial prolongation of physical life with the will of God has been seriously questioned.

Whatever you decide is right for you, do something about it and put your wishes in writing. Make it brief and specific. When living wills were first advocated, it was considered essential to explain the theology or philosophy lying behind them. That is no longer necessary. True, the legal forms offered by hospital associations or law firms are usually written in rather cold legal language. Personally, I recommend giving the document a bit of warmth with your own personal witness of faith. But keep it brief.

It is perfectly permissible to write your own living will or medical power of attorney. However, I strongly suggest using one of the standard forms prepared by a state hospital association or a legal firm. These will be carefully done to comply with the legal code of your home state and will save your doctor or hospital the trouble of a careful analysis to see that all the bases are covered. It is perfectly legal to attach your own testimony as a preamble. To my delight, one of the local legal firms in my community recently provided a document which combines the living will and the medical power of attorney.

For the medical power of attorney, I have counseled those who came to me that husband and wife should name each other as first agent, then one of their children, another family member or a close friend. This provides a certain loving security for husband and wife and gives the necessary support should the spouse no longer be capable of such responsibility or not wish to carry it alone.

Donating One's Organs

Several other items having to do with one's death are worthy of consideration. Would you give your body for medical research as a sort of final bequest to the well-being of humankind? To some this is an attractive final gesture of benevolence and caring. Others may see it differently. Given the present-day high cost of interring the body, it may be attractive to some people. Should you be interested, it is necessary to fill out, sign and file the proper papers.

Many people today agree to donate their organs. This is particularly appropriate in cases of accidental death where various organs have not been damaged by disease. Who knows, your own eyes, kidneys, heart or liver may be the gift of life to some other person. In all sincerity, I have asked several times when this matter was under discussion, "Who would want my eyes after I have used them for some seventy years, and they are showing serious signs of wear?" The reply has been that I should let someone else decide that. To a person whose sight was entirely gone, even my imperfect eyes might be a precious gift. Many states provide a space on drivers' licenses to indicate such willingness.

When You Die, Who Will Know Your Wishes?

A number of years ago after a funeral at which I presided, a fellow minister informed me that he was supposed to have had the sermon. The deceased had verbally requested his services for the occasion shortly before his death. Surprised, I answered that my services had been requested some years before and that the daughters who arranged the funeral were aware of that request and had acted according to their father's directives.

Numerous times people have asked me to preach at their funerals. I have always been careful to answer that the request honors me, and I would be glad to preach for them provided I am still functioning. I am also always careful to suggest that if, indeed, they really wish me to speak, they must communicate their desires to whoever will be in charge of arrangements when they are gone. Otherwise it may be missed.

I don't recall the occasion of this next conversation, but one day I asked a friend whether he had purchased a cemetery lot. He looked surprised and gave a slightly embarrassed laugh, then admitted he had not thought about it. "When I die, someone else will see to my burial."

Actually, it is my opinion, that we do our families a great favor if we have provided a burial lot ahead of time. They will further be glad to know our requests and suggestions for a funeral service. It is best that these be suggestions rather than hard demands because situations change and people come and go. Some things may not be possible or practical after the passing of time.

Some persons even provide their own tombstone ahead of time. Probably most of us would feel a little too modest to be erecting our own monument, but in cases where there is no close family, the idea might be perfectly in order.

Indeed, one of the real kindnesses to the family is to provide information and directions which they will need at the time of your death. Years ago my mother one day called me to her side and showed me a sealed envelope in her Bible. "When I die, come and open this envelope," she instructed me. I remembered and did according to her request. Inside were a testimony of her faith, in the form of a suggested sermon text, and other instructions relating to her funeral. It was all very helpful and comforting.

From my point of view, every individual or every married couple should have a folder of personal and family information filed away. Someone close to them should know where and how to obtain it immediately upon death. It should contain a sheet of vital statistics—full name, date and place of birth, parents' names, including mother's maiden name, marriage date, brothers and sisters living or dead, children living or dead, social security number, educational degrees, offices and titles in church or community. The funeral director will want to know in order to obtain a death certificate, file other necessary legal papers and write a kindly obituary for the local paper. As a pastor serving families in times of bereavement, I have sometimes been surprised how little of this vital information families know or can recall in a time of crisis.

This file should also indicate where to find the key to any lock-boxes at the bank and perhaps other keys as well. It should contain, or tell where to find, titles to vehicles and real estate, financial assets and liabilities, insurance policies, the will and any other legal papers. It is wise to sort through the file about once a year.

Cleaning the Attic

Sometimes I "gross out" my children by remarking that I have one regret about dying, "I won't be here to enjoy the sale." My daughter counters with asking why I don't have a sale while I can be present and just get rid of all the extras I have. That brings me up short with the realization that I do have some sentimental attachment to my "stuff," and I'm not in a hurry to part with it. Besides, the conventional wisdom in my community has it that things bring a better price at an estate sale than a dispersal sale.

Sale or no sale, I do consider it a matter of wholesomely ordering my life, and a kindness to those who follow me, to periodically throw out the trash and keep my house in order. True, I am still accumulating, but I find that this sorting process keeps it somewhat under control. Every year I find things that have become obsolete, things that move out of my area of interest and concern. One word of caution about cleaning out files. If you have ever been an office holder in church or community organizations, you probably have correspondence, minutes or other papers which do not really belong to you personally. At the proper time, these should be returned to the organization or placed in your local church or community archives.

Books are one thing with which I find it hard to deal. Not that I have the kind of sentimental attachment which I develop for some keepsakes, but being a reader and scholar, I always imagine I will have occasion to use any particular book in the not-too-distant future. I must admit that some of my teacher friends have done better at reducing their stock of books upon retirement than I have. Whether it was the sheer necessity of reduced space or a self-discipline superior to mine, I do not know.

Now the very mundane and practical matter of house-cleaning is in a category all by itself. Perhaps the experience of moving to smaller quarters upon retirement is not as bad as we sometimes make it out to be. It forces us to evaluate life and its relationship to things. There can be a measure of dignity and not a little therapy in sorting through one's possessions, giving them a more careful and enlightened evaluation, and being in charge of the decisions to keep, sell, give or throw away. People who are never required to do this may be missing one of life's mature and ennobling disciplines.

Short of the discipline of moving to smaller quarters, I find a certain therapy in just "redding out" the attic or basement. I know there are people who believe that attics belong to eternity and little children on rainy days, therefore should not be disturbed from generation to generation. And there are those who feel that a garage is a status symbol, not necessarily a place to store the family car. Still another reason for not going through our possessions, a sort of delaying tactic, is that our children will want to sort through things when we are gone.

I, on the other hand, propose several reasons why older people should keep a clean house. It promotes awareness, orderliness and a sense of control, all of which are important for the elderly to maintain as long as possible. Secondly, it makes the final sorting task much easier for our children or those appointed to settle our estates. Knowing what we have, where to find it and sharing that knowledge with someone will promote a sense of value and of continuity.

Going through basement or attic usually produces five piles of goods for me: (1) the things I decide to throw away (probably the smallest one), (2) things I keep because they are definitely useful, (3) things that have sentimental value, (4) things that will bring money at an estate sale (this one may hold some surprises), and (5) things about which I just can't decide. At that point, I call my spouse and go over number five cooly and carefully. When it is over, I may not have reduced the contents of the attic greatly, but the place is more orderly. I know better what is there, have a sense of achievement and have made life easier for someone else.

Heirlooms and Keepsakes

Having introduced the idea of heirlooms and keepsakes, I wish to say more. Most of us have some such items that we want to pass along to children, relatives or friends. I have seen some unhappy situations where people thought they were to receive a certain heirloom or gift because of the owner's oral promise. When the person was gone, someone else laid claim to the item.

There are several safeguards to avoid such unpleasantness. Items of great value should be specifically designated in the will. Smaller items should be clearly marked, so there is no mistaking the intentions. I subscribe to an even better idea—give them to the individual you wish to have them while you are living.

One of my aunts spent a large part of her life caring for her parents and finally several older sisters. She acquired a large portion of the family heirlooms, and having some artistic ability in pottery, created some of her own. While still in good health, she gave each of her nieces and nephews an heirloom piece which she chose in keeping with the personality and interests of the receiver. When it came time for her to move out of her house into a small apartment, she had an auction to which only family members were invited—her nieces, nephews and their children. In her case, there were enough of us to make a circle of lively bidders.

The idea of giving away heirlooms while one is still living has much to commend it. For one thing, the giver is in control which is of more and more importance as we grow older. The giving reinforces one's sense of worth and generosity. Then, there is the sheer joy of giving which is a sure way to refresh the springs of life. Finally, it is a sensible way to reduce the crowding and perhaps the care of an overloaded house or apartment.

At our house, we have for a time already been giving the children some of the things they choose as keepsakes, but always with the knowledge and consent of their siblings. Other things are marked with the name of the one who wants to claim them later. Our will also provides that, by common consent and agreed-upon value, any one of our children may claim favored items or even purchase property we own without putting it up at auction. Such provisions, I would say, belong in families where there is an assured measure of love, confidence and good will.

If you really want to do a favor to those who will sort through your things, take all your pictures and snapshots and clearly indicate on the back names of the persons pictured. I wish someone had done that for some of the pictures which have come into my possession.

To be honest, I must admit I have a collection of snapshots from school days of which I can no longer identify all the subjects. Too bad. And while you are sorting through your pictures, it just may be no great loss if you decide to consign some of them to the fire. However, I would warn you not to be rash about this move. Pictures often turn out to have historical value.

Memoirs

Finally, have you thought about writing your memoirs? I know that many people have the urge sometime in life, usually in their later years, to record the events which have shaped their lives and which seem significant to them. Most of us, I suspect, struggle with two conflicting impulses. The first is to say, "But my life was not all that eventful, different or unusual. Why should I record it?" The other is to say, "Life was exciting and significant to me; I would like to share it with my posterity."

Let everyone be assured, "Your life is important." You are a part of family, church and community. Your contribution should not be lost. Here is a small segment of history which you know better than anyone else and to which you have given your own interpretation. Your interpretation of events may differ from that of your siblings or fellow citizens (as people who write memoirs find out), but your interpretation has its own validity and serves to enrich the whole. Your observations and conclusions may well give light to others.

In some cultures—the Chinese, for example—it is considered something of a duty, a final legacy to posterity for the elderly to write down and preserve their own stories, their observations and accumulated wisdom of life. It is true, writing is a discipline and doesn't come easily to most of us. But most of us do have children and grandchildren, nieces and nephews, who will cherish a few mimeographed pages of the most exciting adventures of life—of our own family habits, traditions and jokes. For those who are serious about writing memoirs, I recommend Katie Funk Wiebe's book, *Good Times With Old Times*, as a help in getting started and, indeed, as an interesting book in itself.

There is an interesting metamorphosis that most of us go through regarding our appreciation of family stories and family history. Children like stories, but because of the admonition often accompanying them, children are not initially impressed by stories of the early hours in which Dad had to get up to help with the chores or how many miles he walked to school in the rain and snow. The same is true of mother's stories of how few dresses were in her closet when she went to school or how her family ate turnips instead of potatoes during the Great Depression.

Children need to separate themselves from the parental home, to mature, make their own decisions, climb their own ladder and establish their own identity and place in society. This achieved, these children often return with a new appreciation and relish for the stories of the good old days. Again, this is not to say that children do not like stories nor that the maturation and separation process needs to put a strain on good family relations, though obviously, that sometimes happens.

Esther and I watched with interest, and sometimes trepidation, our daughter's struggle to attain her own identity. She grew up in a small community, went to kindergarten, grade school, high school and two years of college right from her own home. Her mother was a teacher in the local high school, her father taught in the local college and was, first, pastor, then bishop, of all the churches she attended. To make matters worse, her physical resemblance to her dad was a dead give-away. Wherever she introduced herself, it was only one guess as to where she belonged. Obviously, she lived too much under the shadow of her parents.

In the middle of her college career, she decided to make a break for freedom. She took a year off from college and signed on as an exchange trainee in Europe. Soon after her arrival in Europe, she was introduced to a prominent German church leader at a social function. He immediately fixed her with the question, "Would you know Professor L. Wenger? He was one of my teachers when I was in America in school." That encounter probably did more for her father's ego than for her establishment of freedom, at least at the moment.

She survived, safely established her own identity and a professional career and reputation to make her parents proud. Now she is one of my chief boosters, as well as a valued counselor in my attempts at preserving family history.

Remember, your own life is unique and valuable. You occupy a spot in history that no one else can duplicate. Your observations and conclusions are a contribution to the welfare of humankind. To record them for posterity is to extend the benefits of your own life and work.

10. The New Sub-(Super) Culture

They shall still bring forth fruit in old age;
they shall be fresh and flourishing.

(Psalm 92:14)

People who thought
pushing fifty was hard
often find pushing eighty
is easier.

Through the media, I have been learning that the American Association of Retired Persons (AARP) has the most feared and respected lobby in Washington. Congressmen, always with an eye out for re-election, soon learn who butters their bread. The AARP lobby is remarkably well-financed and well-managed. They know what they want, they are vocal and their people have time to go to the polls and vote. While other lobbies may also be well-financed and ably represented, it is the sheer number of senior citizens which gives would-be office-seekers pause. Increasing longevity has fostered an impact on the political arena, a by-product which the fathers of geriatric medicine probably never had in mind.

When President Franklin Roosevelt signed Social Security into law in 1935, he probably did not realize he was creating a new sub-culture. Until that time, retirement was a private matter with no specific age limit indicated and no public benefits attached. Social and economic statistics did not sort out the over-65 group in all the ways we now categorize the population.

More People Are Living Longer

Today people in North America are living longer than they did a hundred years ago and every year the number of persons turning 65 increases. We may approach the statistics by noting that in 1900 there were 3.1 million persons in the United States over 65 years of age. By 1985 there were 28.5 million. To help put this in perspective, note that in 1900 the 65-plus population was 4.1 percent of the total. By 1985 it was 12 percent and is predicted to be 13 percent by the end of this century. A child born in 1900 had a life expectancy of about 48 years. By 1985 life expectancy at birth had risen to 74.7 years.[1]

In our interpretation of these figures, let us remember that medical science first conquered the many diseases of childhood and early adulthood which for generations had prohibited the over-rapid growth of the world population. The recent upsurge in world population figures has, of course, also brought a whole new set of problems. After many of the childhood diseases were brought under control, efforts of medical science were aimed at the degenerative diseases of the older years. Again, great progress was made.

I do not have proven figures for these particular years, but as best I can determine, the life expectancy of persons turning 65 in 1985 is between four and five years longer than the life expectancy of persons turning 65 in 1935 when Social Security became law. Another way of grasping the situation is to note that since 1980, the number of older Americans increased by 11 percent as compared to only a 4 percent increase in the under-65 population. Considering all these figures, one can easily understand that the calculations of the economists and social planners have been severely tested.

With the coming of Social Security in 1935 and the attachment of almost mandatory retirement at 65, a new and very visible segment of the population was created—the elderly, the retired. New categories of statistics were born. The elderly and retired must be counted. Their financial, housing and marital status must be compared with that of the rest of the population, and their demographic direction must be plotted.

A New Way of Life

Of course, this did not all happen at once. Still unfolding, a number of interesting and significant movements have contributed to the phenomenon. First, came the shock of the almost-universal requirement of retirement at 65. Fortunately, that has been somewhat eased. Workers had not planned to retire at 65. In 1935 pensions, medical insurance and social services, as we now know them, had not yet been put in place. Most workers did not have supplemental income over and above Social Security. They were not financially able to retire and still survive with any degree of dignity or maintenance of their customary living standards.

It has taken years for these amenities to be put in place, and the process is never complete. It has likewise taken years for the public to become accustomed to the idea of retirement at 65 and to plan for it financially, psychologically and spiritually. Some people never do.

The visibility of the senior bracket of society has no doubt contributed to the development of the cult of youth at whose shrine America seems to worship. In the workplace, the setting of retirement age has fostered the impression that older workers are less efficient and less competent. Emphasis is placed on youth and vigor, often ignoring the advantages of experience and familiarity of routine. This has led to discrimination against older workers, as they approach the retirement mark.

The myths about the slowing of mental acuity have led to similar discrimination in the professions as well. Fortunately, this myth has been more completely exploded than most of the other myths about aging and, in some professions at least, the elderly have been better able to beat back the assault of the youth cult than has been the case in other places of work.

A third ingredient in the picture is the matter of social imaging. In America, happiness is to be young, beautiful and well-off in terms of possessing the right things. To be old is somehow the denial of all this. The worst handicaps of old age and the most unfortunate of elderly people were made into the stereotype not just of "old age" but of elderly persons. In the minds of many, "old age," therefore an elderly person, is repulsive. This has led to a great deal of discrimination, neglect, simple rudeness, thoughtless behavior and unkind remarks toward those who are older.

Many elderly have risen against this discrimination and negative imaging. The Gray Panthers, American Association of Retired Persons and other organizations have fought back—fought in the courts against discrimination, fought for the economic rights and privileges of the elderly and fought against the negative imaging so hurtful to the dignity of older persons. AARP, now open to all persons above 50 years of age, has a membership of over 22 million. It maintains lobbies in Washington and in state legislatures, working for the Social Security and Medicare benefits of retirees and working to safeguard their pensions and other entitlements.

AARP publishes the magazine *Modern Maturity* aimed at informing and entertaining the retired generation. The organization has been instrumental in securing a number of financial perks for seniors—discounts on merchandise and entertainment, reduced prices on drugs from certain pharmaceutical companies, discounts at hotels and motels and special prices and arrangements on tours. It should be noted that the perks also benefit other Americans as graying America furnishes an attractive market for certain specialized goods and services.

Economic Status of the Elderly

Just what is the financial situation of older Americans? Frankly, the same as every other age bracket. Some are rich, very rich, and some are poor, very poor. As in every other situation, those who are poor and without defense are most susceptible to abuse—they get "ripped off" in the marketplace and often live in fear and seclusion. A few years ago when churches, social agencies and the media "discovered" the plight of the elderly, this particular segment—the needy— became the prototype of what it means to grow old.

When compared with the entire population, the financial situation of the elderly has been improving. In 1985 the poverty rate for the 65-and-older bracket was 12.6 percent as compared with 14.1 percent for the under-65 group. Predictions indicate this trend should continue. This is much different than the situation only ten or twelve years before 1985 when the poverty rate for the elderly was nearly 25 percent. Most recent figures indicate that about 70 percent of older persons live in a family situation while approximately 30 percent live alone. Those who live alone are much more likely to live in poverty and to need help from some outside source. They are also much more likely to be women than men—43 percent of older women live alone as compared with 18 percent of men.

In our society many people need outside help—children, families in financial difficulty, single mothers, abused wives, alcoholics, drug abusers and the elderly. We will never be able to eliminate all the problems or even cover all the needs. Providing care for all these situations will, no doubt, always need to be a prime concern for social agencies and private charities. However, the one population group which seems to have made some improvement, to have been able to do something about its own situation, is the elderly.

Housing for the elderly is a real growth industry in America. True, many retirees wish to keep the "old home" where they raised the family and where children and grandchildren love to come for vacations and all the family get-togethers. But retirement may signal some changes. The house may need some repair and modernizing for greater convenience as housework and maintenance make greater demands on aging muscles. Or it may signal the time to make part of the house into an apartment for additional income and the support of having someone nearby.

Others will prefer to sell the larger house and settle for something smaller, something with less work both outside and inside, providing a greater freedom and mobility.

The real boom in senior housing, however, is in the variety of retirement facilities—condominiums and apartments for purchase or rent. Likewise, there are cottages and apartments designated for government subsidized housing. All these are designed for independent but sheltered living. The degree of shelter may be a matter of choice—security systems, outdoor maintenance, care of major appliances, emergency call systems, freedom from payment of taxes and most monthly bills. This is what more and more older people seem to want and to be able to afford.

At what most of us consider the end of the road, of course, is the nursing home. This has often been a specter confronting the aging. Statistics indicate that approximately 20 percent, one in five persons, will sometime during their life need the services of a nursing facility. However, at any given time, not more than five percent live in such accommodations. With the proliferation of sheltered, but independent, living facilities and with the increasing emphasis on home care and home services, provided either privately or publicly, the specter of the nursing home has somewhat receded.

True, nursing homes that live up to all the horror stories often connected with such places still exist. Thankfully, there are others doing a good job of giving necessary care and, at the same time, making life pleasant, cheerful and full of meaningful activity and entertainment. The problem which still haunts the present generation of retirees, of course, is that such care does not come cheap. Given the present rate of increase among the elderly population, carpenters will be busy for some time to come, building nursing homes and other retirement facilities.

A certain percentage of elderly people will always be desperately poor. Some will be unable to manage their personal affairs, and some will need the physical care of nursing facilities. The thing, however, which best characterizes this new culture of retirees is a fierce independence, a desire to retain control over their own lives. In many ways, they have become their own helpers and advocates.

Old but Active

What do the people of this new sub-culture do? The answer is, "Just about everything that anybody else does." It has been nothing short of amazing the way retirees have become the great American volunteer army. Volunteerism has always been important in our culture. A few years ago, churches and other service agencies were promoting voluntary service for young people. A way of paying a debt to parents and society, of finding their own identity between the idealism of their schooling and demands of the real world and of becoming acquainted with other peoples, many young people volunteered. This was a worthy finish to their education before they settled down to raise their families and do their own time in the business and professional world.

Only very recently have we discovered the vast potential of the newly-created ranks of the retired. Partly out of a growing need for personnel in the area of human services and partly out of the need for retirees themselves to find something significant to do, impressive programs which use retired folks as volunteers have been designed. Volunteer assignments for retirees are scaled to their schedules and endurance levels. Away-from-home assignments are usually for a few weeks or months rather than the one or two years often expected of the youth volunteers.

Here is a vast reservoir of potential volunteers, already possessing skill and experience, who now have time and sometimes money to put into worthy projects. I have friends who volunteered for overseas assignments. Two other couples with whom I am well acquainted have, for a number of years, put in several months of stateside service each winter. They pack their trailer homes and head, one for South Texas, one for Arizona, to work among Latin American immigrants. But many of these people stay right at home finding ways to make their own communities better places to live. Volunteerism has indeed become a hallmark of the retiree culture.

A New Marketing Field

Identification and growth of the elderly population has created a new marketing field which the purveyors of goods and services have not been slow to exploit. When the baby boom subsided and the youth market slowed, the commercial world welcomed retirees to fill in the gap.

Watch the pitch in the slick magazine ads and TV commercials. Watch for the beauty aids—the creams and lotions to smooth away the wrinkles of the women, the jell that brings back the thinning hair of the men and the color which drives away the gray of both. Watch the health ads—vitamins, cereals, arthritis relief, sanitary aids, etc. The clothing market, likewise, thrives on the needs and comforts of senior citizens.

Finally, retirees are the darlings of the travel industry. Young people and families often do their vacationing on a shoestring budget. They buy tents and campers. A surprising number of retirees, on the other hand, have money for leisure travel. Many of them have been planning for it for years. They buy motor homes and tour packages. The TV ads for the Caribbean cruises may show young women splashing into the pool, but the backbone of the ticket desk, particularly the longer cruises to Alaska, Hawaii and the South Pacific is the senior pocketbook. On the bit of travel my wife and I have done to Alaska, Europe and the Middle East, our fellow travelers were, for the most part, retirees like ourselves. The trips were geared to our interests and set to our pace. We loved it.

For those seniors still interested in staying on the cutting edge intellectually, a network of Elderhostels has been developed. These weeklong seminars are sponsored by educational institutions, mostly during the summer. They combine vacation with learning. Their growth over the past few years has been phenomenal and probably has not yet reached its peak.

Where the Action Is

Several decades ago when churches and community agencies discovered the elderly, there was a flurry of activity around the theme, "What can we do for these people?" The idea was to entertain them, make them happy and keep them comfortable. The intentions were wonderful, but the idea backfired. The elderly did not want to be set aside; they did not want simply to be entertained. They wanted to be part of the action—to help with the planning, and particularly in the churches, to continue serving. They wanted to be an integral part of the congregation. Activities for the older folks as a group, yes. But something handed to them on a platter, no.

A task force report to the United Presbyterian Church, USA, in a section entitled "Ministry to and with Aging Persons" notes, and I quote selectively:

Those who are aging can have abundant life as they learn to be less dependent and take greater responsibility for their lives. . .Their marginality frees them not only to see what God is up to, but also to create a new life for themselves. . .Our sensitivity to the liberating dimension of Christ's love leads us to see that the elderly are called to become their own advocates. . .We believe that the elderly are pioneers of a new era of self-reliance and interdependence.[1]

Well said. I have been surprised and heartened at the way the current generation of retirees has asserted itself in the political and economic arenas. Also in the realm of personal and spiritual care and support, I see the more able and more mobile caring for the less able and less fortunate, doing grocery shopping, meeting appointments, helping with correspondence, reading to each other and even just providing companionship, comfort and encouragement. Somewhere I picked up the following idea, "The scattering of family life has this (good) effect—older people are learning to lean upon, to resource one another."

Since a pendulum always swings to the extremes of its trajectory, and since all of us, individuals and groups, tend to become ingrown and self-centered, it may be time for a word of caution. Note that the quotation from the Presbyterian report speaks of self-reliance within interdependence. That interdependence is not to be limited to one age group alone but to intergenerational interdependence as well. The church, of all human institutions, is built on the family model of relationships and on intergenerational wholeness. Some time ago I heard a radio broadcast on which one person raised the complaint that older people in the church are so involved in their own affairs, they are not always there to help those who need their experience. Who would have thought it would come to this?

The marks of this growing sub- or super culture are its identity by age and status, its growing political power, its singular place in the economy—by amassed savings and purchasing power—and the structure of its interdependence. When by age and by law, even by a measure of discrimination, you are obliged to come down off your ladder, it is no longer true that you have no place to stand.

11. Please Hold My Ladder

The silver-haired head is a crown of glory,
if it is found in the way of righteousness.

(Proverbs 16:31)

Everyone
wants to live
a long time,
but no one wants to be old.

The thesis of my book is that happiness lies pretty much in our own hands. Most of us are about as happy as we make up our minds to be. Our sense of self-worth and self-confidence cannot be handed to us by someone else. We must work it out in the process of living. It is not so much what happens to us as how we react to what happens, that determines both the quantity of our happiness and the quality of our characters.

While I do stand by my thesis, psychology has amply demonstrated that the treatment we receive from other people and the impressions they give us of ourselves also make a difference. When we are young, parents and teachers can make or break our self-esteem. The approval or disapproval of friends serves as a yardstick for our self-confidence. Again in older years, when we may have doubts about our capacities, a word of encouragement will go a long way in building the degree of self-worth which we eventually achieve.

Retirement Shock

Retirement is a milestone in every life—an event that triggers a lot of introspection, a lot of evaluation and an assessment of successes and failures. From the moment of retirement, we are put in a different category. We belong to the older generation. Many times we feel suddenly old by definition rather than by years or by any physical decline. With good reason, we fight against it.

Understanding what is happening—that much of it is arbitrary or by definition rather than actual—helps keep things in perspective. Surviving that first shock of retirement, when our world suddenly changes, depends on a number of things. Perhaps first, is simply being aware of what is "out there"—of the adjustments we will need to make, the attitudes toward old age and the prejudices we will encounter. Secondly, our survival will depend on the preparations we have made, mentally and physically, for the years to come—a place to live, our work involvement, our social and religious activity. Finally, our philosophical and religious understanding and acceptance of the meaning of life determine how we view our experiences. We accept that life moves on from generation to generation, that sickness and decline are the common lot of humankind, that death itself is a part of life. Even retirement and the transfer of power and responsibility are fundamentally right, though often ineptly administered.

It is only fair to say that life could be made a great deal easier, happier and more pleasant. The strains and pains of aging could be greatly diminished if popular attitudes toward the elderly and the prejudices which these attitudes engender could be changed. As an older person, you may elect to devote your energies toward fighting ageism, prejudice directed toward the elderly and the poverty sometimes imposed upon older people. But don't put off your own happiness until these inequities have been conquered. It will doubtless be a long time. Rather, learn to live with and above these undesirable elements.

At the same time, we have reason to be glad for the social, political and economic progress which we have made in changing public attitudes and bettering our own state. And let us say with gratitude that many churches and social agencies are working diligently to relieve present distress among the more disadvantaged elderly, to change the prevailing mindset about what it means to be old and to help persons of whatever age prepare for their own inevitable aging. Praise the Lord for what is being done and the people who have the vision and courage to work for change.

Beauty Is More Than Skin Deep

One thing we might well dispense with, to the benefit of both young and old, is the American cult of youth worship. In its clutches the young look forward with fear and the old look back with regret, so that neither can concentrate on the enjoyment of the present. The purveyors of the youth culture have sold the American public a false bill of goods. The first dogma proclaims that beauty is linked to youth. Its graces are smooth skin, silken hair, sparkling eyes and shapely limbs. These, of course, must be enhanced with the proper embellishments of expensive ornaments, lavish make-up and stylish clothes. No one in the youth cult would dare acknowledge the beauty of the mature physical body or the grace and poise which come only with experience. Do not be unaware that inner peace, love, acceptance, tolerance and concern translate themselves into an outward glow more permanent than the cosmetic beauty of the current pageant queen.

A second false dogma suggests that all joy and pleasure, all enjoyment of life, disappear as the bloom of youth fades. Older people are believed to be restricted in their eating, no longer able to appreciate the pleasures of restaurant meals and other fine dinners. Supposedly, they can no longer engage in active sports or enjoy any kind of play. Most of all, the rumors have it that older persons are no longer capable of any sexual activity or pleasure. To lay this myth to rest would be a favor to the elderly and would remove a major source of fear for the young.

A third error is the dogma of senility. According to this one, all older persons lose their mental sharpness. Supposedly beginning as early as age 30, people in their seventies are considered completely out of touch with the real world. In a large measure, this attitude on the part of the young reflects their own fear. Everybody wants to live a long time, but nobody wants to be old. Unfortunately, the stereotype of old age comes from that small percentage of the population whose faculties deteriorate earliest and whose poverty denies them proper care and shelter from public gaze. Conveniently by-passed are those millions of retirees who spend their days in useful employment and satisfying social enjoyment, even though it be with a more measured tread.

How Old Do You Want to Be?

An elderly gentleman in a mixed social gathering was probed to reveal his age. When he acknowledged his 90 years, an impertinent youth snorted, "Who wants to be 90?" The answer, of course, is nobody and everybody. Like Augustine who prayed, "Lord, make me holy—but not now," we have created a culture where everyone wants to live long but everyone also fears old age. Spare those of us who have grown older the pitying looks, the snide remarks and the media publicity that says life belongs only to the young.

I was particularly intrigued with the turn of a phrase used by a speaker who recently addressed a retiree group which I regularly attend. He referred to the advantages which we possess because we had been young longer than so many around us who thought they knew the answers to life's questions. Or, as someone else put it, we know more about being young than our youthful disdainers know about being old.

Not quite all the motivation of this movement comes from the hidden fear of the young themselves. Economic factors also enter in. The advertising media, at the behest of the market moguls, has sold a "bill of youth" with all the beauty aids, the right clothes, the drinks, the sports cars and the beach parties to keep it going.

Just yesterday I was anxiously trying to help one of my few remaining aunts up the steps into her house (with her walker). She brushed my offers aside with a smiling, "I can do it. Just see how spry I am. I want to do that as long as I can." Bravo. That is the kind of triumph which few of the youth cult know anything about as yet.

Ageism—Its Cruelties

A word much in vogue by writers on the problems of the elderly is ageism. While the cult of youth worship exalts the young, ageism practices discrimination against older persons. There is a subtle notion afoot that after reaching a given number of years—usually retirement—we suddenly become non-persons, or at least persons of a different kind. For some strange and unexplainable reason, we no longer merit the same respect, prompt service and polite deference which "normal" people receive. At its worst, the impression is left that we do not feel, or at least are not supposed to feel, the slights and put-downs which we receive.

One of the first places where those who are advancing in years feel discrimination is in the job market. Even those approaching retirement find it difficult to get new jobs. At sixty-five, it becomes well nigh impossible. According to conventional wisdom, the "oldies" can no longer learn new skills, their physical and mental powers have diminished and short-term workers mess up financial planning. Even those approaching retirement within a few years find the odds stacked against them if they become unemployed or need to change jobs.

Strangely enough, the elderly also find themselves discriminated against in the marketplace. In stores and shops, older persons find that clerks have less time for them and do not as readily make efforts to find the goods most suitable and pleasing to them. In the check-out line, there is little patience and too few helpful words for the older person who may be a bit slower in figuring things out or understanding instructions. This has been amply documented by social workers who first went shopping disguised as an older person and later followed the same track with the disguise removed.

Everybody admires and humors a baby. Babies may drool, throw things on the floor or wet their pants. People smile indulgently and take it in stride. But let an old person drool, drop something or have an accident, and the response is a show of revulsion. What is the difference? The most likely explanation revolves around that same element of fear and denial. Younger people see in the elderly what they fear they will become. They do not want to look at it. The reaction may really not be a deliberate unkindness but an unconscious denial and flight from reality.

The good news is that many of the people now reaching retirement age will enjoy good health and comfortable mobility for many years and may even escape this embarrassing discrimination. That anyone, even those who exhibit more noticeably the physical deterioration of old age, should suffer such thoughtless discrimination for the simple crime of having lived too many years—and that at the hands of those who are following in their footsteps—is the sad part.

My mother used to tell a story—probably made up to teach children respect for their elders—about the man who became so irritated with his old father, whose trembling hands spilled food on the table, that he finally made, or bought, a wooden bowl for the father's use and put him at a little table by himself. One day the man found his own small son in the barn hammering away at some boards he had cut.

"What are you making, son?" asked the father.

"Why, Daddy," replied the boy, "I'm making a pig trough for you to use when you get old like Grandpa." Needless to say, the old grandfather was soon restored to his rightful place.

Fruitless Denial

A few years ago my alma mater proposed an organization of those who had been graduated for fifty years. There would be honorary dinners and reminiscent gatherings. At commencement time, we would march in the academic parade and, among other good things, receive recognition. The organizing committee suggested the name, "Old Grads." Immediately there was a murmur of conflicting opinions about the name. A dozen or more alternates were suggested, most of them aimed at eliminating, or at least softening, the designation "old."

Well, we finally adopted the original suggestion, over some loud protests. The incident riveted in my mind how universal is our fear and denial of that most common of all human phenomena—growing older. The struggle to find ways to talk about aging which do not hurt goes on constantly. People once grew old, now we become elderly. We once reached old age, now we never get beyond aging. It is proper to reach adulthood, but then we cling to it by advancing only to mature adults or older adults. We seemed to have arrived when someone invented senior citizens, but soon we had golden-agers and keen-agers. One of my teenage buddies used to say in a slightly different context, "I don't care what they call me, just so they call me three times a day." Whether old or young, we have certain fears, certain feelings, certain preferences. It is only fair, wise and kind that we deal gently with one another and respect each other's feelings so far as possible. Regardless of the designation we prefer, all of us who live long enough eventually pass over that unseen line into old age.

There are also those descriptions intentionally designed to degrade and to hurt. They should be avoided by caring persons. The "old biddy" and "old geezer" epithets carry connotations of being a busybody or a rascal. The older person who manifests any awareness of sex is unfairly in danger of being labeled a slut or a dirty old man. Even the sometimes well-intentioned "little old lady" can hurt, giving the impression of a resigned helplessness and dependence. Some years ago I became aware of the "grand old man" syndrome. At first I thought it sounded rather nice and complimentary. Further observation, however, changed my mind somewhat. It can be a subtle device to keep someone with charisma in place. The grand old man is supposed to smile benignly on the foibles of the youthful set. He is not to expose his wisdom or offer advice to those in authority. Above all, he does not rock the boat of the current establishment. I'm not sure I even want to be a "grand old man!"

The Need to Be Involved

One thing common to all ages and every stage of life is the desire to be involved. The most severe burden borne by the handicapped is usually the sense of being different; of being set aside and excluded from the company of others and the normal activities of life. Something very similar to that occurs at retirement for many persons. They are suddenly set aside— no longer able to exercise their skills. Their counsel is no longer sought. They feel wounded.

For many, no doubt, a feeling of ambivalence sets in. The desire to savor the newfound freedom of retirement is dampened by a sense of loss and exclusion. Beyond a doubt, the rigidity with which retirement is often enforced robs many of the opportunity for continued usefulness and their sense of dignity. It likewise robs the community of valuable resources in the accumulated skills and wisdom of the elderly.

I have a special word for churches and church institutions— for local congregations in particular. For the business and professional community, retirement has its legal and financial implications which tend to give it finality. Churches and church institutions have done little better than the secular world in softening the blow of retirement and its subsequent loss of status and involvement. For millions of Christians, the church is not only the teacher and mediator of salvation, it is also a haven of refuge from all human hurts and disappointments. From the church there should be no retirement. Yet even here the elderly often feel pushed aside, denied the dignity and opportunity of service which they have long given from the heart as an offering to the Lord.

Of course, in the church, as anywhere else in society, the generations come and go. One generation deals with its problems and serves its time. The next generation must be given its place and assume its responsibility. But in the church, as nowhere else, this transition should be achieved with grace and kindness. There should be a full measure of recognition of human dignity. There should be something of worth to do so long as there is the desire and the physical ability. Older persons might serve as counselors, as elder members of committees, where they might be at liberty to come or go as their strength indicated, or as ex officio members of boards.

I knew a man who served his congregation for many years and in a number of capacities. For years he was a trustee and took great pride in the upkeep of grounds and facilities. When age finally seemed to indicate that some younger person should be put in his place, he was distraught. While his reaction may have been extreme, a wise and kind pastor suggested that he be designated trustee emeritus. It gave recognition and allowed him to stay in touch with what was going on. The arrangement was good for him and for the congregation.

Of all society's institutions, the church stands to lose most by prematurely cutting off the devoted service and silencing the voice of experience and the accumulated wisdom of its elders.

Something has gone wrong with the concept of retirement in American culture. Instead of being a rite of passage, it becomes for many a sort of dead-end street. Of course, there are celebrations, gifts or engraved plaques and speeches of praise and congratulations. A lot of nice things are said that nobody took time (or dared) say before. For about three days, the retiree lives in euphoria. Then the reality begins to dawn. He or she has been cut off from life as they knew it and left to their own devices. To renew life, find new friends, new activities and sources of meaning is not easy. Of course, the thesis of this book has been that one should be working on those things long before retirement day comes. Perhaps, however, society should not put so much of that burden on the individual.

A friend of mine once said that the longest walk he ever took was from the back of the church where his "Married Men's" Sunday school class met to the front of the sanctuary where the "Old Men's" class convened. The reason—he felt this was his last promotion. From that class there was no place to go but to the cemetery.

Most other events in life are considered rites of passage—beginning school, baptism, confirmation, bar mitzvah, graduation, marriage, parenthood. All of these bring honor and prestige and signal good things to come. Why cannot retirement be such a rite of passage? In the ancient Middle East when a man had finished his years of physical labor, he joined the council of the elders, sitting in the gates of the city. His badge of honor was his white hair and flowing beard. He was respected for his years and his accumulated wisdom. Formally or informally, he gave counsel and judgment on the everyday affairs of the people. Some primitive tribes continue to practice such a system. In America there is too little respect for old age, too little opportunity given to harvest its fruits. Could not something be done to make retirement a rite of passage?

12. If I Have Learned to Live

But at evening time it shall happen
that it will be light.

(Zechariah 14:7b)

The price of sin has never gone up,
but the cost has always been too high to pay.

Years ago in the old Guernsey Barn in Lancaster County, I heard the musical, *Strangers at the Mill*. There was one snatch of song which I have never forgotten:

> It hardly matters what I know,
> From where I came or when I go,
> Or whom I must forgive.
>
> It hardly matters how I die,
> Or whom I am remembered by,
> If I have learned to live.[1]

I know this is not a biblical text, but it sounds like something I could use to make a sermon. If I have learned to live. It comes to me as an admonition and a challenge. A challenge to find joy and meaning in life, to make some contribution to the happiness and well-being of those whom my life touches in whatever time and place it is cast.

A relatively small percentage of all the persons born into the world will ever have their statues adorning the world's parliamentary halls or have their busts displayed in the libraries of the world's educational institutions. Only a few will find their names in the lights above the world's entertainment palaces or in the sports' halls of fame. Not many will be invited to send their resume to *Who's Who*.

Suppose you are now sixty or seventy years old. How many of the "famous" people of the world can you now name, and which of them do you envy? As you remember your reading of history or the current news gossip, how many of these persons were really happy or seem to have been satisfied and fulfilled?

With what person whom you now know would you like to trade places? Sure, most of us do plenty of griping. We complain about our misfortunes and unfair treatment. But when the chips are down, with whom would we want to trade places? Most people, comparing themselves with those they know in their own cultural circle, would prefer to keep their own troubles rather than trade with some other person's seeming good fortune. As one of my teachers (which one I now forget) once said, "I would rather live with my questions than with most people's answers." All this is to say that our own personal identity is a great gift and a precious possession.

Living and Forgiving

If I am asked to name the one most important element in learning to live the confident, peaceful and well-adjusted life, it is the ability to forgive. In the Christian context, the way is plain. We can and should forgive because we have been forgiven of God. "And be kind to one another, tenderhearted, forgiving one another, just as God in Christ also forgave you" (Ephesians 4:32). Or the even more forthright words of Jesus, "For if you forgive men their trespasses, your Heavenly Father will also forgive you. But if you do not forgive men their trespasses, neither will your Father forgive your trespasses" (Matthew 6:14-15). It is not that God is mean or demanding, rather our own unforgiving spirit shuts God's forgiveness and peace out of our lives.

None of us will be so fortunate as to go through life without needing to exercise forgiveness. Perhaps none of us should, for to miss the opportunity and the discipline of learning and practicing forgiveness would certainly leave us with a large facet of our character undeveloped. Life will always have pain. We are cheated in some financial deal, misrepresented in our intentions or passed over in the distribution of honors. Can we forgive and move on, or do we elect to carry a grudge?

Many of us have also experienced major life-scarring events—childhood abuse, character maliciously attacked and defamed, betrayal by one we trusted in a way that leaves us wounded and bleeding. For these we may need counseling and enlightened understanding before we know what and how to forgive. In any of these situations, both the power and the mandate to forgive lies in God's forgiveness of us. To learn to forgive is to learn to live, in the sense that living is a joyous and confident experience.

In the course of my ministry, I have had to deal with a few persons who simply refused to lay down a quarrel. They continued to demand settlement on their terms (which probably would not have made them happy) and elected to carry a grudge. I felt sorry and defeated that neither my counseling and entreaties nor that of others could persuade them to be, on the one hand, reasonable, nor on the other, forgiving. I could only feel sorry for them because they were persons from whom the joy of life and the spirit of living seemed to have departed.

I will share one very poignant experience out of my own life because in the end it became a means of growth and of understanding toward others. In the midst of busy administrative duties, I came into a three-way tangle involving two other men with whom I needed to work intimately. I was embarrassed and hurt. Putting the best construction on the situation, I had been badly misunderstood. At worst it looked like somebody was out to get me. I needed to make some resolution if I was to function effectively and happily.

All this happened about the time psychiatrists were telling us the right way to handle hurt is by direct confrontation—to tell it like it is, have an audience with the offending party and pour out your hurt, to say you are angry; a sort of Matthew 18 gone to seed. The problem was I could not secure an audience. I felt I was getting the run-around. The responsible parties were being evasive and refused to face the issue. My frustration grew by leaps and bounds.

Finally, I sought out a Christian psychiatrist whom I trusted and told him my story, even proposing my own solution. "Aren't there times," I asked, "when the only thing to do is to forgive, even though the offender has not asked your forgiveness, even though you have not had the opportunity to express your hurt?"

My friend agreed. "For the Christian," he said, "there are such times. Jesus did it, and He has made it possible for us."

I told myself I would forgive. In prayer I told the Lord I would forgive, and asked His help. The hurt did not go away at once, but I persisted in my forgiveness and gradually it became real. I knew I had forgiven when some months, perhaps a year later, something happened to call the whole episode to my attention. I turned it over in my mind and suddenly I said to myself, "Look, I am thinking about this, and I am not even hurting. Praise the Lord!" In forgiveness there is liberty. In forgiveness there is living.

Faith for Living

One of the magazines I read is *Mature Living*, a Baptist publication primarily for older adults. Mostly stories and easy reading, it chronicles those events in the life of the writers which have given them their memories, their understanding and their appreciation of people. It is strong on building faith in God, who gives life meaning through everyday events of sorrow, joy, disappointment and happy surprise.

Just as important as forgiving and being forgiven is what I call the life of faith. It is a biblical expression, and I really don't know which should have been discussed first—forgiveness or faith. Faith involves, first of all, the assurance of the forgiveness of sin, a commitment to follow Christ in true discipleship and deliverance from the fear of death. With these things settled, one can learn to live.

I know that many people try to make settlement with life outside of Christian faith. Through some humanistic philosophy, they settle on the meaning of life or else accept that it has no meaning. Their goals may be pleasure and success. They might even include benevolence in their list of desirable actions. Seeing the inevitability of death, they may also be resigned to this fate. Many are good and respectable people. But I wonder if they have really learned to live. True meaning in life I find only in the Christian context where learning to live is not only for personal joy but for the happiness of others and the glory of Christ—where living is not only for time but eternity as well.

Learning to live calls for the frank understanding that life is never easy and not always fair. Jesus never promised His followers that they would be delivered from trouble, only that He would be with them. Life is made up of joy and sorrow, success and failure, sunshine and shadow. Too much of failure and sorrow can break the spirit. Too much of ease and success can give a distorted view of the reality of life.

Beyond doubt, faith is the most frequent and familiar biblical description of the man or woman who has learned the way of life—to live by faith, to achieve through faith and yes, to die in faith. It is our privilege to know that "all things work together for good to them that love God" (Romans 8:28). But do not be carried away by my exuberance. The life of faith is not an automatic or easy thing. Our faith will be tried by life's sorrows, temptations and betrayals. Learning to live by faith is a lifelong challenge.

Faith Testing in Older Years

There are problems, challenges and victories peculiar to growing older. We should note some of the spiritual problems of aging. Sometimes the young hold the fond perception that at least one of the benefits of growing old is that life becomes serene and easy. The temptations of the flesh fade away and doubts disappear. A lovely idealism, we may occasionally see older persons who seem to be approaching it, but, like John Wesley's complete sanctification, none quite dare to claim it. In fact, quite the contrary is often true. The spiritual battles of older years can be very rough. Conventional wisdom says certain temptations are common to youth and others common to old age. I call that a very broad rule of thumb. Anger, pride, untruthfulness, lust and other bodily appetites do not go away with years but only as we put to death the works of the flesh by the power of the Spirit.

There are, it is true, certain spiritual trials and temptations which are common to growing older and of which pastors should be aware in their ministry to the elderly. There is the inevitable physical decline. It is hard to accept the fact that we no longer function as we once did. There may be illness and times of prolonged pain. Eventually the loss of mobility and control of daily affairs may even take a corresponding toll on spiritual vitality almost unknown to the individual.

Somewhere along the way of growing older, most individuals review the years, tasting again their joys and sorrows in a more contemplative way, no longer pushing them aside in the rush of present activity. In doing this, they may uncover old griefs—the loss of children by death or betrayal by a trusted friend which drastically affected their lives. They may need to work through these losses again in a new way. It is a time, also, when many persons revive their real or imagined failures in life.

One frequent source of imagined failures has to do with children. If children have somehow turned out to be a disappointment, parents may spend time agonizing over, "What did we do wrong?" Such feelings of guilt are always futile and, for the most part, unjustified. Other disappointments may come back to loom as personal failures evoking feelings of guilt. Occasionally, a survey of years may leave the feeling that "I didn't accomplish much; if I had another chance, I would do better."

Frequently, in the experience of older persons, the "sins of their youth" come back to haunt. Things which had been "confessed and made right" may return to disturb peace and assurance, even to create doubt of salvation.

Many, many times these feelings of guilt and regret have no just cause for existence—at least not now. They may be the result of too much time to think on the past and not enough focus on the future. Nevertheless, these feelings are very real and very disturbing, and they need to be met. Most older people have more time on their hands than they once did. One of the best ways to put such time to use is in Bible reading and prayer. My own personal Bible reading has become a source of joy and strength to me in my retirement. This is often the perfect answer to feelings of guilt and failure.

People often desire as well the opportunity to talk things over with an understanding pastor, a trusted friend or a support group. The church should be very sensitive to these needs. Somewhere, somehow, these persons, though they have been Christians for many years, should have the opportunity as they feel the need to again make confessions, declare anew their faith and renew their dedication to Christ. This is ever so much better than the glib assurance of pastor or nurse, "O don't worry, you're a good person; everything is all right."

Now let me say, I understand perfectly well that all of us have those things in our lives which we wish we did not need to remember. There are some things we would do differently, some words we wish we could somehow reach out and recall. There may be bitter memories of unfairness that came our way. When inclined to think on these, we should have the good sense to balance them out with the memories of success, of kindness given and received—the simple joys of daily living in family, church and community. To learn to live is to accept life's joys and sorrows, successes and failures, disappointments and surprises, wrongs done and wrongs received, knowing that for inequities given there is forgiveness, and for inequities received there is recompense, and that life goes on now and forever.

Lest I seem to be giving mixed signals, let me elaborate. I said earlier that I believe older people are entitled to some leisure, some time to reminisce, to review life and to put things together. I also warned that for a certain number "too much time to think" could produce negative results—guilt, bitterness, even fear of death.

Recently I read *Winter Grace* by Kathleen Fischer. I was delighted to find her articulating some of the very ideas which had been on my own mind. Fischer referred to one of the last public appearances of Dorothy Day in which Day spoke of the universal need of repentance and forgiveness. These are often the desired fruit of those searching memories and musings of the older years.

Fischer also cites psychiatrist Robert N. Butler and others who have given a great deal of study to this habit of reviewing memories on the part of older persons. It is not simply a passing of the time in idleness, a longing for the "good old days" as we often suppose. Our memories tell us who and what we are. Actually reviewing these memories, putting life together is, or should be, a healing process. Some psychiatrists link this review of memories with a final preparation for death.[2]

Reviewing our lives and sorting out our memories can result in a clearer vision of the whole of life. For many it will lead to a putting away of guilt, a resolution of inner conflicts, even restoration of broken relationships. In this process a trusted friend and counselor is often great help.

Finally, to avoid the unhappy negative results—depression, bitterness and cynicism—that a review of memories may produce, it must be done from a faith perspective—from the knowledge that life is not always fair and only God is always provident and good.

Happiness or Joy

In the days when my work with school and church required frequent traveling, I often engaged the waitresses in restaurants with the question, "Are you happy today?" Though often surprised, they usually gave an affirmative answer. My next question, "What right do you have to be happy?" often floored them. I believe that from the beginning God intended for everyone to be happy. Happy in the enjoyment of a beautiful and bountiful creation, happy in the companionship of fellow beings and happy in the fellowship of the Creator.

With the experience of sin, all that changed. Gone was the intimate relationship with the Creator. Gone the mutual trust between human beings. In its place suspicion, greed and violence, even to death, took over. Gone was a beautiful creation without briars and thistles. The possibilities of happiness had disappeared.

In such a world we may rightfully ask, "What is happiness?" "Where is it to be found?" and "Who has a right to be happy?" But God does not give up easily, and in a way of saying it, neither does humankind. God set about providing a way (in Christ) whereby people could be restored in right relationship with Him and, in consequence, to right relationship with their fellows. The right and possibility of gathering happiness was restored.

Since meanings are often attached to words, happiness has most often come to mean the things that make us feel good, as "happiness is a warm puppy." To be happy is to laugh and smile, to experience titillation. Some people are afraid of happiness as though it would bring bad luck. I remember a parishioner telling me with sadness how his parents curbed his youthful expressions of happiness. If he got up whistling in the morning, one of them would say, "The cat will catch that bird before night." The curbing of his youthful impulses to happiness indeed seemed to have affected his whole life.

A word which some prefer over happiness to describe these emotions is joy. Joy is a Christian virtue and indicates a deep underlying peace and confidence which enables us to face life with understanding and acceptance. It lifts our spirit above the trials and troubles of the day to an eternal hope. We can experience both sorrow and joy at the same time. I think I understand the technical or theological difference between happiness and joy, but I like to keep the meaning of the two close together, and I want to promote the gathering and storing of happiness (happy memories) from youth to old age.

Happiness for the sake of happiness is not an end in itself. For example, I do not have a right to be happy to the exclusion of happiness for others. Edith Wharton once said, "If only we'd stop trying to be happy, we could have a pretty good time." Happiness is rather the by-product of right living, of making possible happiness for others. In happiness we extract the good and the joyful from each situation and contact. Perhaps I am being overly idealistic. In the August-September 1989 issue of *Sunburst*, Ann Bender writes, "Many people, no matter what age, have feelings of sadness and depression. None of us can be happy all the time."[3] I certainly agree that none of us are happy all the time. But I am sure that all of us could be happy more of the time than we are. I still feel sorry for my friend whose parents repressed his impulse to happiness as a child. All of us develop patterns of living in youth that will determine the character of our old age.

In her book, *If You Do Love Old Men*, Virginia Owens tells the story of her grandfather, a man of fierce independence and deep suspicions regarding the motives of others. As he became older, his traits were more firmly fixed. Communication with him became more difficult and reasoning well-nigh impossible. In one episode, the old man blamed his son-in-law for breaking down one of his peach trees. His daughter tried to placate him. Gently at first, then with rising frustration, she reasoned with him, all to no avail. Finally, in utter desperation she stopped, looked at her agitated father and, in disbelief, asked herself, "Who is this person? Is he sick? Is he crazy? Or is this the way he has always been, secretly bitter and full of rage?"[4]

The truth is people do not become this way because they are old. It is just that they no longer are able, or no longer try, to hide it. People do not become old and cranky, but cranky people become old. The traits of character we cultivate in youth will simply be accentuated in old age whether they are good or bad.

Cultivating Happy Memories

Of particular importance in learning to live, in preparing for a happy and fruitful old age, is the cultivation of good memories. Somewhere I read that the mind has a faculty of collecting the good and the pleasant for storage. The painful memories are gradually sorted out and discarded. Of course, there are those perverse minds which choose to collect the painful, the disappointing, the failures. Such people are the ones who give old age a bad name. Esther and I frequently visit a nearby nursing home. I must admit that on the surface of things, it is not a very cheerful place to visit, but I am impressed with the number of cheerful people I meet there.

To promote good and cheerful memories, I have decided to share some of my own. While I know they will not stir the same emotions in you which they stir in me, I hope this recitation will arouse for each of you memories of your own. Some memories are life-forming, setting our directions and destiny. Others, like an old scrapbook, drop splashes of sunshine along the way.

I remember the security of my own parental home, the guidance that came more by example than verbal teaching. One of my earliest memories is of sitting by the kitchen window on winter evenings while my mother prepared supper.

The window looked out to the west where I saw the creek that ran through the meadow, the rolling hills of neighboring farms and the dark line of the distant mountain with the everchanging clouds above it, touched with the last rays of the winter sun. Those clouds have not ceased to fascinate me.

I remember the white country church, shaded by tall Lombardy poplars, where my parents took me. I remember the people I met there, my Sunday school teachers and pastors who, along with my parents, taught me the way of salvation and influenced me in such a way that my life has been spent about the work of the church.

I am grateful for that very special young woman who responded to my attentions and consented to be my wife. I am grateful for the fifty years God has given us to love and to share together in satisfying service in the church. Sure, we had our rough spots, but an abiding love and confidence, a shared purpose in life, carried us through these years with a deepening appreciation and enjoyment of each other.

I am grateful for the three children who came to gladden our lives and to challenge our skills of parenting. They are equally precious each one. But if the two younger will pardon me, I must recall the thrill of holding that first one in my arms—flesh of my flesh, the fruit of our love—and later, to hold him on my lap while his soft lips explored my face and his breath caressed my cheek.

There are memories of a different type—the vivid snapshots which stand out for happy recollection out of the everyday experiences of the years. I remember the biggest whirlwind I ever saw. I'll grant that whirlwinds of the Shenandoah Valley probably can't match those of the Great Plains, but on this autumn day while I followed a team of horses across a dusty field, the wind began to pick up the fallen leaves from the cottonwoods along the creek. In a wide vortex, larger than any

I have seen before or since, the leaves were carried hundreds of feet into the sky. I can still see them.

I remember the morning just before dawn, as I searched the pasture for the cows to bring them in for milking, when suddenly the sky just above me was lit up with dozens of meteors. Approaching at different angles, they were so close I could hear a swish like the wind as they advanced. Their brilliant trails remained, glowing in the sky, for several minutes after they were gone. I stood shivering in amazement and fear. I wish I could see it again.

I remember the day I discovered snow rollers by the hundreds on a neighboring hillside. Snow rollers are wind-blown snow balls, shaped like a muff. These varied in size from that of a thimble to a half-bushel measure. I knew it had to be something rare, and later my search of nature journals yielded a description and explanation. I also learned that "once in a lifetime" was anyone's quota. I have never seen this phenomenon again.

I remember the day on our honeymoon, when traveling down the coastal highway in California, my wife and I stopped at the edge of a cliff high above the Pacific Ocean. There we sat in quiet contentment, contemplating the sun-filled expanse of sky and sea, which in the distance seemed perfectly calm but at its edge broke upon the beach in foaming waves. And there just behind the breakers were the dolphins leaping and playing. The scene has been fifty years etched on my memory and shows no sign of fading. Another encounter with dolphins happened while I was fishing in the Chesapeake Bay with several preacher buddies. Our attention was attracted by a school of dolphins, moving down the bay in a follow-the-leader fashion and leaping as they went. From a little distance, they had the appearance of a half-mile of living croquet hoops protruding from the water.

I remember much more, but these are sufficient to illustrate what I mean by gathering memories to live by in older years. Don't think that I could not dredge up some painful and embarrassing memories. I certainly could, and I hope that I learned from those painful experiences. But at seventy-eight, they do not seem nearly so important to remember as the pleasant and beautiful ones.

> It hardly matters how I die,
> Or whom I am remembered by,
> If I have learned to live.

This book has been about living well, even to old age, about learning to live happily, even in old age. It is about making a contribution to life—family, church and community. It is about making the world a little better and then leaving it gladly to those who follow after.

In my time as a minister, I have conducted funerals for persons of all ages. We always feel some sense of tragedy when someone dies young—and yet, how many years does it take to make a full life? We philosophize (correctly) that it is not how long we live but how well we live that is important. For most of us, our death will not make national news. The local paper will take note of the event. Our families and friends will gather to remember and to say kind things about us. Naturally, the circle of persons will be larger for some than for others, but even that is not important. Remember how that sharp young lawyer asked Jesus, "Who is my neighbor?" Instead of a direct answer, Jesus told a story that gave His hearers to understand that the neighbor is one whom our own life touches, one to whom we have the opportunity to do good. And when we have done that, our life has been full, we have learned to live and to die. Several years ago at a conference on aging which I helped plan, we took for our slogan, "May you live as long as you want to and want to as long as you live."

Lately I have taken up what some may consider a rather morbid pastime. In the obituary column of our local newspaper, I note the ages of those who have died. I do the same for the obituaries in the weekly edition of my denominational church paper. According to my little game, if more have died who are my age or younger, then I am ahead. If more of those who died were older than I, then I am behind. I haven't actually kept records, but my running observation is that in the newspaper, which covers the entire community of people, I am easily ahead. The average age of death is somewhat younger than my 78 years. In the church paper, which records a more restricted group of professing Christians, I am behind. The average age of death is higher.

This little game confirms my belief. Christian faith, which promotes clean and wholesome living and reduces many of the fears and stresses which plague humankind, including the fear of death, is the primary ingredient in the formula for learning to live.

NOTES

Chapter 1

1. *AARP—A Profile of Older Americans* (1992), p. 1.
2. Eli A. Rubinstein, "The Not So Golden Years," *Newsweek* (Oct. 7, 1991), p. 13.

Chapter 3

1. Samuel Gerber, *Learning to Die* (Scottdale, Pa.: Herald Press, 1984), p. 74.

Chapter 4

1. "Lead Me Gently Home," Words and music by W.L. Thompson.

Chapter 5

1. Elise Maclay, *Green Winter: Celebrations of Later Life* (Henry Holt and Company, Inc., 1990).

Chapter 8

1. Henry W. Longfellow, "My Lost Youth," *Three Centuries of American Poetry and Prose* (Scott, Foresman & Co., 1917), p. 626.
2. "Life Events Scale" developed by Dr. Thomas A. Holmes, psychiatrist, and his colleagues at the University of Washington School of Medicine at Seattle.
3. *AARP—A Profile of Older Americans* (1992).
4. Edwin Markham, "Lincoln, Man of the People," *11011 Famous Poems* (Chicago: The Cable Co., 1929), p. 159.
5. "Never Alone," Words by Eben E. Rexford and music by M.L. McPhail.

Chapter 10

1. United Presbyterian Church USA, Report of Ad Hoc Committee on "Ministry to and with Aging Persons," Appendix 2, "Abundant Life for Aging People."

Chapter 12

1. Merle Good, *Strangers at the Mill* (Lancaster, PA.: Merle Good, 1968).
2. Kathleen Fischer, *Winter Grace* (New York: Paulist Press 1985), pp. 6, 37.
3. Ann Bender, *Sunburst* (Aug.-Sept. 1989).
4. Virginia Owens, *If You Do Love Old Men* (Grand Rapids: William B. Eerdmans, 1990), p. 56.

Bibliography

Brown, Paul Fremont. *From Here to Retirement.* Waco, Texas: Word
 Books, 1988.
Comfort, Alex. *Say Yes to Old Age.* New York: Crown Publishers, 1990.
Fischer, Kathleen. *Winter Grace.* New York: Paulist Press, 1985.
Gerber, Samuel, translated by Peter Dyck. *Learning to Die.* Scottdale,
 Pennsylvania: Herald Press, 1984.
Hein, Marvin. *Like a Shock of Wheat.* Scottdale, Pennsylvania: Herald
 Press, 1981.
Howe, Ruel L. *How to Stay Younger While Growing Older.* Waco,
 Texas: Word Books, 1974.
Hutchison, Frank. *Aging Comes of Age.* Louisville, Kentucky:
 Westminster/John Knox Press, 1991.
Johnson, Eric W. *Older and Wiser.* New York: Walker and Company,
 1986.
Kerr, Horace L. *How to Minister to Senior Adults in Your Church.*
 Nashville: Broadman Press, 1980.
Manning, Doug. *When Love Gets Tough.* Hereford, Texas: In-Sight
 Books, 1985.
Maclay, Elise. *Green Winter.* New York: Henry Holt and Compnay,
 Inc., 1990.
Maves, Paul B. *Faith for the Older Years.* Minneapolis: Augsburg
 Publishing House, 1986.
Nouwen, Henry J. and Walter J. Gaffney. *Aging.* New York:
 Doubleday/Image Books, 1990.
Owens, Virginia Stem. *If You Do Love Old Men.* Grand Rapids:
 William B. Eerdmans, 1990.
Schmitt, Abraham. *Dialogue with Death.* Waco, Texas: Word Books,
 1976.
Smith, Tilman R. *In Favor of Growing Older.* Scottdale, Pennsylvania:
 Herald Press, 1981.
Wiebe, Katie Funk. *Good Times With Old Times.* Scottdale,
 Pennsylvania: Herald Press, 1979.

Other Sources
AARP. "A Profile of Older Americans." Washington: Program
 Resources Dept., AARP, 1989, 1992 Reports.
United Presbyterian Church USA, Report of Ad Hoc Committee on
 "Ministry to and with Aging Persons," Appendix 2, "Abundant
 Life for Aging People."

About the Author

Born in the Shenandoah Valley of Virginia, Linden M. Wenger (pictured on cover) grew up on a small farm where he acquired an abiding appreciation of the natural world.

He graduated from Eastern Mennonite College with a degree in Bible and received his B.D. and Th.M. from Union Theological Seminary, Richmond, Virginia. He did advanced studies at Princeton and with New York University Land of the Bible Workshop in Israel.

In 1941 he married Esther Huber of Lancaster, Pennsylvania. The Wengers have three grown children. After Linden was ordained to the ministry in 1945, they spent ten years in the West Virginia hills where he pastored several churches.

Beginning in 1955, he spent 23 years as Associate Professor of Bible and Philosophy at Eastern Mennonite College and Seminary while continuing in the work of church administration. Ordained bishop in 1959, Wenger was overseer of the Northern District of Virginia Conference until his retirement in 1985. He held various offices in the Virginia Conference and in the old Mennonite General Conference. Since retirement he has chaired the Virginia Conference Older Adults Ministries Committee. He also contributes to various Mennonite Church periodicals.